HOUSE OF DEBT

HOUSE OF DEBT

HOW THEY (AND YOU) CAUSED THE
GREAT RECESSION, AND HOW WE CAN PREVENT IT
FROM HAPPENING AGAIN

ATIF MIAN AND AMIR SUFI

The University of Chicago Press   Chicago and London

Atif Mian is professor of economics and public policy
at Princeton University.
Amir Sufi is the Chicago Board of Trade Professor of Finance
at the University of Chicago Booth School of Business.

The University of Chicago Press, Chicago 60637
The University of Chicago Press, Ltd., London
© 2014 by Atif Mian and Amir Sufi
All rights reserved. Published 2014.
Printed in the United States of America

23 22 21 20 19 18 17 16 15 14   2 3 4 5

ISBN-13: 978-0-226-08194-6 (cloth)
ISBN-13: 978-0-226-13864-0 (e-book)
DOI: 10.7208/chicago/9780226138640.001.0001

Library of Congress Cataloging-in-Publication Data

Mian, Atif, 1975– author.
House of debt: how they (and you) caused the Great Recession,
and how we can prevent it from happening again / Atif Mian
and Amir Sufi.
pages; cm
Includes bibliographical references and index.
ISBN 978-0-226-08194-6 (cloth: alk. paper) —
ISBN 978-0-226-13864-0 (e-book) 1. Financial crises—United
States. 2. Consumer credit—United States. 3. Debtor and creditor—
United States. 4. Foreclosure—United States. 5. Financial crises—
Prevention. 6. Foreclosure—United States—Prevention. 7. Global
Financial Crisis, 2008–2009. I. Sufi, Amir, author. II. Title.
HB3743.M53 2014
330.973'0931—dc23   2013049671

♾ This paper meets the requirements of ANSI/NISO Z39.48-1992
(Permanence of Paper).

To our parents, for always being there
To Saima and Ayesha

CONTENTS

1: A SCANDAL IN BOHEMIA

Selling recreational vehicles used to be easy in America. As a button worn by Winnebago CEO Bob Olson read, "You can't take sex, booze, or weekends away from the American people." But things went horribly wrong in 2008, when sales for Monaco Coach Corporation, a giant in the RV industry, plummeted by almost 30 percent. This left Monaco management with little choice. Craig Wanichek, their spokesman, lamented, "We are sad that the economic environment, obviously outside our control, has forced us to make . . . difficult decisions."

Monaco was the number-one producer of diesel-powered motor homes. They had a long history in northern Indiana making vehicles that were sold throughout the United States. In 2005, the company sold over 15,000 vehicles and employed about 3,000 people in Wakarusa, Nappanee, and Elkhart Counties in Indiana. In July 2008, 1,430 workers at two Indiana plants of Monaco Coach Corporation were let go. Employees were stunned. Jennifer Eiler, who worked at the plant in Wakarusa County, spoke to a reporter at a restaurant down the road: "I was very shocked. We thought there could be another layoff, but we did not expect this." Karen Hundt, a bartender at a hotel in Wakarusa, summed up the difficulties faced by laid-off workers: "It's all these people have done for years. Who's going to hire them when they are in their 50s? They are just in shock. A lot of it hasn't hit them yet."

In 2008 this painful episode played out repeatedly throughout northern Indiana. By the end of the year, the unemployment rate in Elkhart, Indiana, had jumped from 4.9 to 16.2 percent. Almost twenty thousand jobs were lost. And the effects of unemployment were felt in schools and charities throughout the region. Soup kitchens in Elkhart saw twice as many people showing up for free meals, and the Salvation Army saw a jump in demand for food and toys during the Christmas season. About 60 percent of students in the Elkhart public schools system had low-enough family income to qualify for the free-lunch program.[1]

Northern Indiana felt the pain early, but it certainly wasn't alone. The Great American Recession swept away 8 million jobs between 2007 and 2009. More than 4 million homes were foreclosed. If it weren't for the Great Recession, the income of the United States in 2012 would have been higher by $2 trillion, around $17,000 per household.[2] The deeper human costs are even more severe. Study after study points to the significant negative psychological effects of unemployment, including depression and even suicide. Workers who are laid off during recessions lose on average three full years of lifetime income potential.[3] Franklin Delano Roosevelt articulated the devastation quite accurately by calling unemployment "the greatest menace to our social order."[4]

Just like workers at the Monaco plants in Indiana, innocent bystanders losing their jobs during recessions often feel shocked, stunned, and confused. And for good reason. Severe economic contractions are in many ways a mystery. They are almost never instigated by any obvious destruction of the economy's capacity to produce. In the Great Recession, for example, there was no natural disaster or war that destroyed buildings, machines, or the latest cutting-edge technologies. Workers at Monaco did not suddenly lose the vast knowledge they had acquired over years of training. The economy sputtered, spending collapsed, and millions of jobs were lost. The human costs of severe economic contractions are undoubtedly immense. But there is no obvious reason why they happen.

Intense pain makes people rush to the doctor for answers. Why am I experiencing this pain? What can I do to alleviate it? To feel better, we are willing to take medicine or change our lifestyle. When it comes to economic pain, who do we go to for answers? How do we get well? Unfortunately, people don't hold economists in the same esteem as doctors. Writing in the 1930s during the Great Depression, John Maynard Keynes criticized his fellow economists for being "unmoved by the lack of correspondence between the results of their theory and the facts of observation." And as a result, the ordinary man has a "growing unwillingness to accord to economists that measure of respect which he gives to other groups of scientists whose theoretical results are confirmed with observation when they are applied to the facts."[5]

There has been an explosion in data on economic activity and advancement in the techniques we can use to evaluate them, which gives us a huge advantage over Keynes and his contemporaries. Still, our goal in this book is ambitious. We seek to use data and scientific methods to answer some of the most important questions facing the modern economy: Why do severe recessions happen? Could we have prevented the Great Recession and its consequences? How can we prevent such crises? This book provides answers to these questions based on empirical evidence. Laid-off workers at Monaco, like millions of other Americans who lost their jobs, deserve an evidence-based explanation for why the Great Recession occurred, and what we can do to avoid more of them in the future.

Whodunit?

In "A Scandal in Bohemia," Sherlock Holmes famously remarks that "it is a capital mistake to theorize before one has data. Insensibly one begins to twist facts to suit theories, instead of theories to suit facts."[6] The mystery of economic disasters presents a challenge on par with anything the great detective faced. It is easy for economists to fall prey to theorizing before they have a good understanding of

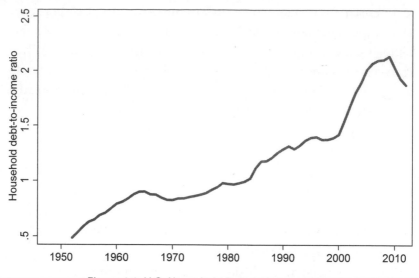

Figure 1.1: U.S. Household Debt-to-Income Ratio

the evidence, but our approach must resemble Sherlock Holmes's. Let's begin by collecting as many facts as possible.

When it comes to the Great Recession, one important fact jumps out: the United States witnessed a dramatic rise in household debt between 2000 and 2007—the total amount *doubled* in these seven years to $14 trillion, and the household debt-to-income ratio skyrocketed from 1.4 to 2.1. To put this in perspective, figure 1.1 shows the U.S. household debt-to-income ratio from 1950 to 2010. Debt rose steadily to 2000, then there was a sharp change.

Using a longer historical pattern (based on the household-debt-to-GDP [gross domestic product] ratio), economist David Beim showed that the increase prior to the Great Recession is matched by only one other episode in the last century of U.S. history: the initial years of the Great Depression.[7] From 1920 to 1929, there was an explosion in both mortgage debt and installment debt for purchasing automobiles and furniture. The data are less precise, but calculations done in 1930 by the economist Charles Persons suggest that outstanding mortgages for urban nonfarm properties *tripled* from 1920 to 1929.[8] Such a massive increase in mortgage debt even swamps the housing-boom years of 2000–2007.

The rise in installment financing in the 1920s revolutionized the manner in which households purchased durable goods, items like washing machines, cars, and furniture. Martha Olney, a leading expert on the history of consumer credit, explains that "the 1920s mark the crucial turning point in the history of consumer credit."[9] For the first time in U.S. history, merchants selling durable goods began to assume that a potential buyer walking through their door would use debt to purchase. Society's attitudes toward borrowing had changed, and purchasing on credit became more acceptable.

With this increased willingness to lend to consumers, household spending in the 1920s rose faster than income.[10] Consumer debt as a percentage of household income more than doubled during the ten years before the Great Depression, and scholars have documented an "unusually large buildup of household liabilities in 1929."[11] Persons, writing in 1930, was unambiguous in his conclusions regarding debt in the 1920s: "The past decade has witnessed a great volume of credit inflation. Our period of prosperity in part was based on nothing more substantial than debt expansion."[12] And as households loaded up on debt to purchase new products, they saved less. Olney estimates that the personal savings rate for the United States fell from 7.1 percent between 1898 and 1916 to 4.4 percent from 1922 to 1929.

So one fact we observe is that both the Great Recession and Great Depression were preceded by a large run-up in household debt. There is another striking commonality: both started off with a mysteriously large drop in household spending. Workers at Monaco Coach Corporation understood this well. They were let go in large part because of the sharp decline in motor-home purchases in 2007 and 2008. The pattern was widespread. Purchases of durable goods like autos, furniture, and appliances plummeted early in the Great Recession—before the worst of the financial crisis in September 2008. Auto sales from January to August 2008 were down almost 10 percent compared to 2007, also before the worst part of the recession or financial crisis.

The Great Depression also began with a large drop in household spending. Economic historian Peter Temin holds that "the Depression was severe because the fall in autonomous spending was large and sustained," and he remarks further that the consumption decline in 1930 was "truly autonomous," or too big to be explained by falling income and prices. Just as in the Great Recession, the drop in spending that set off the Great Depression was mysteriously large.[13]

The International Evidence

This pattern of large jumps in household debt and drops in spending preceding economic disasters isn't unique to the United States. Evidence demonstrates that this relation is robust internationally. And looking internationally, we notice something else: the bigger the increase in debt, the harder the fall in spending. A 2010 study of the Great Recession in the sixteen OECD (Organisation for Economic Co-operation and Development) countries by Reuven Glick and Kevin Lansing shows that countries with the largest increase in household debt from 1997 to 2007 were exactly the ones that suffered the largest decline in household spending from 2008 to 2009.[14] The authors find a strong correlation between household-debt growth before the downturn and the decline in consumption during the Great Recession. As they note, consumption fell most sharply in Ireland and Denmark, two countries that witnessed enormous increases in household debt in the early 2000s. As striking as the increase in household debt was in the United States from 2000 to 2007, the increase was even larger in Ireland, Denmark, Norway, the United Kingdom, Spain, Portugal, and the Netherlands. And as dramatic as the decline in household spending was in the United States, it was even larger in five of these six countries (the exception was Portugal).

A study by researchers at the International Monetary Fund (IMF) expands the Glick and Lansing sample to thirty-six countries, bringing in many eastern European and Asian countries, and focuses on data through 2010.[15] Their findings confirm that growth in household debt is one of the best predictors of the decline in household spending during the recession. The basic argument put forward in these studies is simple: If you had known how much household debt had increased in a country *prior* to the Great Recession, you would have been able to predict exactly which countries would have the most severe decline in spending *during* the Great Recession.

But is the relation between household-debt growth and recession severity unique to the Great Recession? In 1994, long before the Great Recession, Mervyn King, the recent governor of the Bank of England, gave a presidential address to the European Economic Association titled "Debt Deflation: Theory and Evidence." In the very first line of the abstract, he argued: "In the early 1990s the most severe recessions occurred in those countries which had experienced the largest increase in private debt burdens."[16] In the address, he documented the relation between the growth in household debt in a given country from 1984 to 1988 and the country's decline in economic growth from 1989 to 1992. This was analogous to the analysis that Glick and Lansing and the IMF researchers gave twenty years later for the Great Recession. Despite focusing on a completely different recession, King found exactly the same relation: Countries with the largest increase in household-debt burdens—Sweden and the United Kingdom, in particular—experienced the largest decline in growth during the recession.

Another set of economic downturns we can examine are what economists Carmen Reinhart and Kenneth Rogoff call the "big five" postwar banking crises in the developed world: Spain in 1977, Norway in 1987, Finland and Sweden in 1991, and Japan in 1992.[17] These recessions were triggered by asset-price collapses that led to massive losses in the banking sector, and all were especially deep downturns with slow recoveries. Reinhart and Rogoff show that all five episodes were preceded by large run-ups in real-estate prices and large increases in the current-account deficits (the amount borrowed by the country as a whole from foreigners) of the countries.

But Reinhart and Rogoff don't emphasize the household-debt patterns that preceded the banking crises. To shed some light on the household-debt patterns, Moritz Schularick and Alan Taylor put together an excellent data set that covers all of these episodes except Finland. In the remaining four, the banking crises emphasized by Reinhart and Rogoff were all preceded by large run-ups in private-debt burdens. (By private debt, we mean the debt of households and non-financial firms, instead of the debt of the government or banks.) These banking crises were in a sense also private-debt crises—they were all preceded by large run-ups in private debt, just as with the Great Recession and the Great Depression in the United States. So banking crises and large run-ups in household debt are closely related—their combination catalyzes financial crises, and the groundbreaking research of Reinhart and Rogoff demonstrates that they are associated with the most severe economic downturns.[18] While banking crises may be acute events that capture people's attention, we must also recognize the run-ups in household debt that precede them.

Which aspect of a financial crisis is more important in determining the severity of a recession: the run-up in private-debt burdens or the banking crisis? Research by Oscar Jorda, Moritz Schularick, and Alan Taylor helps answer this question.[19] They looked at over two hundred recessions in fourteen advanced countries between 1870 and 2008. They begin by confirming the basic Reinhart and Rogoff pattern: Banking-crisis recessions are much more severe than normal recessions. But Jorda, Schularick, and Taylor also find that banking-crisis recessions are preceded by a much larger increase in private debt than other recessions. In fact, the expansion in debt is *five times* as large before a banking-crisis recession. Also, banking-crisis recessions with low levels of private debt are similar to normal recessions. So, without elevated levels of debt, banking-crisis recessions are unexceptional. They also demonstrate that normal recessions with high private debt are more severe than other normal recessions. Even if there is no banking crisis, elevated levels of private debt make recessions worse. However, they show that the worst recessions include both high private debt and a banking crisis.[20] The conclusion drawn by Jorda, Schularick, and Taylor from their analysis of a huge sample of recessions is direct:

> We document, to our knowledge for the first time, that throughout a century or more of modern economic history in advanced countries *a close relationship has existed between the build-up of credit during an expansion and the severity of the subsequent recession.* . . . [W]e show that *the economic costs of financial crises can vary considerably depending on the leverage incurred during the previous expansion phase* [our emphasis].[21]

Taken together, both the international and U.S. evidence reveals a strong pattern: *Economic disasters are almost always preceded by a large increase in household debt.* In fact, the correlation is so robust that it is as close to an empirical law as it gets in macroeconomics. Further, large increases in household debt and economic disasters seem to be linked by collapses in spending.

So an initial look at the evidence suggests a link between household debt, spending, and severe recessions. But the exact relation between the three is not precisely clear. This allows for alternative explanations, and many intelligent and respected economists have looked elsewhere. They argue that household debt is largely a sideshow—not the main attraction when it comes to explaining severe recessions.

The Alternative Views

Those economists who are suspicious of the importance of household debt usually have some alternative in mind. Perhaps the most common is the *fundamentals* view, according to which severe recessions are caused by some fundamental shock to the economy: a natural disaster, a political coup, or a change in expectations of growth in the future.

But most severe recessions we've discussed above were not preceded by some obvious act of nature or political disaster. As a result, the fundamentals view usually blames a change in expectations of growth, in which the run-up in debt before a recession merely reflects optimistic expectations that income or productivity will grow. Perhaps there is some technology that people believe will lead to huge improvements in well-being. Severe recession results when these high expectations are not realized. People lose faith that technology will advance or that incomes will improve, and therefore they spend less. In the fundamentals view, debt still increases before severe recessions. But the correlation is spurious—it is not indicative of a causal relation.

A second explanation is the *animal spirits* view, in which economic fluctuations are driven by irrational and volatile beliefs. It is similar to the fundamentals view except that these beliefs are not the result of any rational process. For example, during the housing boom before the Great Recession, people may have irrationally thought that house prices would rise forever. Then fickle human nature led to a dramatic revision of beliefs. People became pessimistic and cut back on spending. House prices collapsed, and the economy went into a tailspin because of a self-fulfilling prophecy. People got scared of a downturn, and their fear made the downturn inevitable. Once again, in this view household debt had little to do with the ensuing downturn. In both the fundamentals and animal-spirits mind-sets, there is a strong sense of fatalism: a large drop in economic activity cannot be predicted or avoided. We simply have to accept them as a natural part of the economic process.

A third hypothesis often put forward is the *banking* view, which holds that the central problem with the economy is a severely weakened financial sector that has stopped the flow of credit. According to this, the run-up in debt is not a problem; the problem is that we've stopped the flow of debt. If we can just get banks to start lending to households and businesses again, everything will be all right. If we save the banks, we will save the economy. Everything will go back to normal.

The banking view in particular enjoyed an immense amount of support among policy makers during the Great Recession. On September 24, 2008, President George W. Bush expressed his great enthusiasm for it in a hallmark speech outlining his administration's response.[22] As he saw it, "Financial assets related to home mortgages have lost value during the house decline, and the banks holding these assets have restricted credit. As a result, our entire economy is in danger. . . . So I propose that the federal government reduce the risk posed by these troubled assets and supply urgently needed money so banks and other financial institutions can avoid collapse and resume lending. . . . This rescue effort . . . is aimed at preserving America's overall economy." If we save the banks, he argued, it would help "create jobs" and it "will help our economy grow." There's no such thing as excessive debt—instead, we should encourage banks to lend even more.

*   *   *

The only way we can address—and perhaps even prevent—economic catastrophes is by understanding their causes. During the Great Recession, disagreement on causes overshadowed the facts that policy makers desperately needed to clean up the mess. We must distinguish whether there is something more to the link between household debt and severe recessions or if the alternatives above are true. The best way to test this is the scientific method: let's take a close look at the data and see which theory is valid. That is the purpose of this book.

To pin down exactly how household debt affects the economy, we zero in on the United States during the Great Recession. We have a major advantage over economists who lived through prior recessions thanks to the recent explosion in data availability and computing power. We now have microeconomic data on an abundance of outcomes, including borrowing, spending, house prices, and defaults. All of these data are available at the zip-code level for the United States, and some are available even at the individual level. This allows us to examine who had more debt and who cut back on spending—and who lost their jobs.

The Big Picture

As it turns out, we think debt is dangerous. If this is correct, and large increases in household debt really do generate severe recessions, we must fundamentally rethink the financial system. One of the main purposes of financial markets is to help people in the economy share risk. The financial system offers many products that reduce risk: life insurance, a portfolio of stocks, or put options on a major index. Households need a sense of security that they are protected against unforeseen events.

A financial system that thrives on the massive use of debt by households does exactly what we don't want it do—it concentrates risk squarely on the debtor. We want the financial system to insure us against shocks like a decline in house prices. But instead, as we will show, it concentrates the losses on home owners. The financial system actually works *against* us, not *for* us. For home owners with a mortgage, for example, we will demonstrate how home equity is much riskier than the mortgage held by the bank, something many home owners realize only when house prices collapse.

But it's not all bad news. If we are correct that excessive reliance on debt is in fact our culprit, it is a problem that potentially can be fixed. We don't need to view severe recessions and mass unemployment as an inevitable part of the business cycle. We can determine our own economic fate. We hope that the end result of this book is that it will provide an intellectual framework, strongly supported by evidence, that can help us respond to future recessions— and even prevent them. We understand this is an ambitious goal.

But we must pursue it. We strongly believe that recessions are not inevitable—they are not mysterious acts of nature that we must accept. Instead, recessions are a product of a financial system that fosters too much household debt. Economic disasters are *man-made*, and the right framework can help us understand how to prevent them.

PART I
BUSTED

2: DEBT AND DESTRUCTION

All of us face unforeseen threats that can alter our lives: an unexpected illness, a horrible storm, a fire. We understand we need to be protected against such events, and we buy insurance to be compensated when these events happen. This is one of the most common ways we interact with financial markets. It is far better for the financial system as a whole to bear these risks than any one individual.

One of us (Amir) grew up in Topeka, Kansas, where the threat of tornadoes has long been hardwired in people's minds. From an early age, Kansans go through tornado drills in schools. Kids pour out of classrooms into hallways and are taught to curl up into a ball next to the wall with their hands covering their heads and necks. These drills are done at least twice a year; school administrators know they must be prepared for a tornado striking out of the blue. Similarly, home owners in Kansas prepare for tornadoes by making sure their insurance policy will pay them if, God forbid, their home is destroyed in a tornado. Money can't make up for the loss of one's home, but it ensures that a family can begin rebuilding their lives during such a desperate time. Insurance *protects* people—this is one of the primary roles of the financial system.

A collapse in house prices, while presumably not dangerous in terms of injury or death, presents another serious unforeseen risk to home owners. For many Americans, home equity is their only source of wealth. They may be counting on it to retire or to help pay for a child's college education. A dramatic decline in house prices is just as unexpected as a tornado barreling down on a small town in Kansas. But when it comes to the risk associated with house prices, the financial system's reliance on mortgage debt does the exact opposite of insurance: it concentrates the risk on the home owner. While insurance protects the home owner, debt puts the home owner at risk. Here's how.

The Harshness of Debt

Debt plays such a common role in the economy that we often forget how harsh it is. The fundamental feature of debt is that the borrower must bear the first losses associated with a decline in asset prices. For example, if a home owner buys a home worth $100,000 using an $80,000 mortgage, then the home owner's equity in the home is $20,000. If house prices drop 20 percent, the home owner loses $20,000—their full investment—while the mortgage lender escapes unscathed. If the home owner sells the home for the new price of $80,000, they must use the full proceeds to pay off the mortgage. They walk away with nothing. In the jargon of finance, the mortgage lender has the *senior claim* on the home and is therefore protected if house prices decline. The home owner has the *junior claim* and experiences huge losses if house prices decline.

But we shouldn't think of the mortgage lender in this example as an independent entity. The mortgage lender uses money from *savers* in the economy. Savers give money to the bank either as deposits, debt, or equity, and are therefore the ultimate owners of the mortgage bank. When we say that the mortgage lender has the senior claim on the home, what we really mean is that savers in the economy have the senior claim on the home. Savers, who have high net worth, are protected against house-price declines much more than borrowers.

Now let's take a step back and consider the entire economy of borrowers and savers. When house prices in the aggregate collapse by 20 percent, the losses are concentrated on the borrowers in the economy. Given that borrowers already had low net worth before the crash (which is why they needed to borrow), the concentration of losses on them devastates their financial condition. They already had very little net worth—now they have even less. In contrast, the savers, who typically have a lot of financial assets and little mortgage debt, experience a much less severe decline in their net worth when house prices fall. This is because they ultimately own—through their deposits, bonds, and equity holdings—the senior claims on houses in the economy. House prices may fall so far that even the senior claims take losses, but they are much less severe than the devastation wrought on the borrowers.

Hence, the concentration of losses on debtors is inextricably linked to wealth inequality. When house prices collapse in an economy with high debt levels, the collapse amplifies wealth inequality because low net-worth households bear the lion's share of the losses. While savers are also negatively impacted, their relative position actually improves. In the example above, before the crash savers owned 80 percent of the home whereas the home owner owned 20 percent. After the crash, the home owner is completely wiped out, and savers own 100 percent of the home.

Debt and Wealth Inequality in the Great Recession

During the Great Recession, house prices fell $5.5 trillion—this was enormous, especially considering the annual economic output of the U.S. economy is roughly $14 trillion. Given such a massive hit, the net worth of home owners obviously suffered. But what was the *distribution* of those losses: how worse off were borrowers, actually?

Let's start with an examination of the net-worth distribution in the United States in 2007.[1] A household's net worth is composed of two main types of assets: financial assets and housing assets. Financial assets include stocks, bonds, checking and savings deposits, and other business interests a household owns. Net worth is defined to be financial assets plus housing assets, minus any debt. Mortgages and home-equity debt are by far the most important components of household debt, making up 80 percent of all household debt as of 2006.

In 2007 there were dramatic differences across U.S. households in both the composition of net worth and leverage (amount of debt). Home owners in the bottom 20 percent of the net-worth distribution—the poorest home owners—were highly levered. Their leverage ratio, or, the ratio of total debt to total assets, was near 80 percent (as in the example above with a house worth $100,000). Moreover, the poorest home owners relied almost exclusively on home equity in their net worth. About $4 out of every $5 of net worth was in home equity, so poor home owners had almost no financial assets going into the recession. They had only home equity, and it was highly levered.

The rich were different in two important ways. First, they had a lot less debt coming into the recession. The richest 20 percent of home owners had a leverage ratio of only 7 percent, compared to the 80 percent leverage ratio of the poorest home owners. Second, their net worth was overwhelmingly concentrated in non-housing assets. While the poor had $4 of home equity for every $1 of other assets, the rich were exactly the opposite, with $1 of home equity for every $4 of other assets, like money-market funds, stocks, and bonds. Figure 2.1 shows these facts graphically. It splits home owners in the United States in 2007 into five quintiles based on net worth, with the poorest households on the left side of the graph and the richest on the right. The figure illustrates the fraction of total assets each of the five quintiles had in debt, home equity, and financial wealth. As we move to the right of the graph, we can see how leverage declines and financial wealth increases.

This isn't surprising. A poor man's debt is a rich man's asset. Since it is ultimately the rich who are lending to the poor through the financial system, as we move from poor home owners to rich home owners, debt declines and financial assets rise. As we mentioned above, the use of debt and wealth inequality are closely

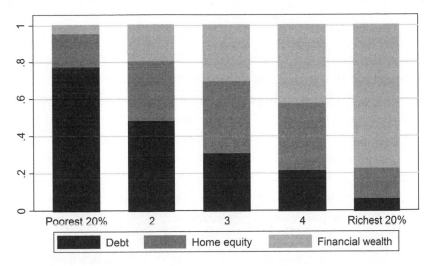

Figure 2.1: Leverage Ratio for Home Owners, 2007, by Net Worth Quintile

linked. There is nothing sinister about the rich financing the poor. But it is crucial to remember that this lending takes the form of *debt financing*. When the rich own the stocks and bonds of a bank, they in turn own the mortgages the bank has made, and interest payments from home owners flow through the financial system to the rich.

Figure 2.1 summarizes key facts that are important to keep in mind as we enter the discussion of the recession. The poorest home owners were the most levered and the most exposed to the risks of the housing sector, and they owned almost no financial assets. The combination of high leverage, high exposure to housing, and little financial wealth would prove disastrous for the households who were the weakest.

How the Poor Got Poorer

From 2006 to 2009, house prices for the nation as a whole fell 30 percent. And they stayed low, only barely recovering toward the end of 2012. The S&P 500, a measure of stock prices, fell dramatically during 2008 and early 2009, but rebounded strongly afterward. Bond prices, as measured by the Vanguard Total Bond Market Index, experienced a strong rally throughout the recession as market interest rates plummeted—from 2007 to 2012, bond prices rose by more than 30 percent. Any household that held bonds coming into the Great Recession had a fantastic hedge against the economic collapse. But, as we have shown above, only the richest households in the economy owned bonds.

The collapse in house prices hit low net-worth households the hardest because their wealth was tied exclusively to home equity. But this tells only part of the story. The fact that low net-worth households had very high debt burdens amplified the destruction of their net worth. This amplification is the *leverage multiplier*. The leverage multiplier describes mathematically how a decline in house prices leads to a larger decline in net worth for a household with leverage.

To see it at work, let's return to the example we've been using, where a home owner has 20 percent equity in a home worth $100,000, and therefore a loan-to-value ratio of 80 percent (and therefore an $80,000 mortgage). If house prices fall 20 percent, what is the percent decline in the home owner's equity in the home? Here's a hint: it's much larger than 20 percent! The home owner had $20,000 in equity before the drop in house prices. When the prices drop, the house is only worth $80,000. But the mortgage is still $80,000, which means that the home owner's equity has been completely wiped out—a 100 percent decline. In this example, the leverage multiplier was 5. A 20 percent decline in house prices led to a decline in the home owner's equity of 100 percent, five times larger.[2]

From 2006 to 2009, house prices across the country fell by 30 percent. But since poor home owners were levered, their net worth fell by much more. In fact, because low net-worth home owners had a leverage ratio of 80 percent, a 30 percent decline in house prices completely wiped out their entire net worth. This is a fact often overlooked: when we say house prices fell by 30 percent, the decline in net worth for indebted home owners was much larger because of the leverage multiplier.

Taken together, these facts tell us exactly which home owners were hit hardest by the Great Recession. Poor home owners had almost no financial assets; their wealth consisted almost entirely of home equity. Further, their home equity was the junior claim. So the decline in house prices was multiplied by a significant leverage multiplier. While financial assets recovered, poor households saw nothing from these gains.

Figure 2.2 puts these facts together and shows one of the most important patterns of the Great Recession. It illustrates the evolution of household net worth for the bottom quintile, the middle quintile, and the highest quintile of the home-owner wealth distribution. The net worth of poor home owners was absolutely hammered during the Great Recession. From 2007 to 2010, their net worth collapsed from $30,000 to almost zero. This is the leverage multiplier at work. The decline in net worth during the Great Recession completely erased all the gains from 1992 to 2007. This is exactly what we would predict given the reliance on home equity and their large amount of debt. The average net worth of rich home owners declined from $3.2 million to $2.9 million. While the dollar amount of losses was considerable, the percentage decline was negligible—they were hardly touched. The decline wasn't even large enough to offset any of the gains from 1992 to 2004. The rich made out well because they held financial assets that performed much better during the recession than housing. And many of the financial assets were senior claims on houses.

High debt in combination with the dramatic decline in house prices increased the already large gap between the rich and poor in the United States. Yes, the poor were poor to begin with, but they lost everything because debt concentrated overall house-price declines directly on their net worth. This is a fundamental feature of debt: it imposes enormous losses on exactly the households that have the least. Those with the most are left in a much better relative

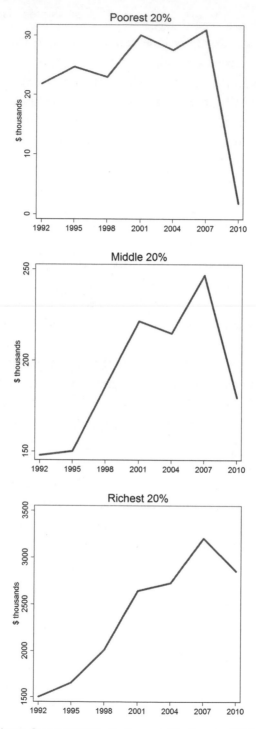

Figure 2.2: Home-Owner Net Worth, Poorest, Median, and Richest Quintiles

position because of their senior claim on the assets in the economy. Inequality was already severe in the United States before the recession. In 2007 the top 10 percent of the net-worth distribution had 71 percent of the wealth in the economy. This was up from 66 percent in 1992. In 2010 the share of the top 10 percent jumped to 74 percent, which is consistent with the patterns shown above. The rich stayed rich while the poor got poorer.

Many have discussed trends in income and wealth inequality, but they usually overlook the role of debt. A financial system that relies excessively on debt amplifies wealth inequality. While there is much to learn about the causes of inequality by looking into the role of debt, our focus is on how the uneven distribution of losses affects the entire economy.

The Geography of Net-Worth Destruction

The crash in house prices during the Great Recession had a strong geographic component, and our research relies on this.[3] The counties with the sharpest drops in net worth were located in California and Florida. Other pockets of the country also had very large drops, including counties in Colorado, Maryland, and Minnesota. Counties in the middle of the country, such as those in Kansas, Oklahoma, and Texas, largely escaped the housing collapse.

In some areas of the country, the decline in housing net worth was stunning. In four counties in the Central Valley of northern California—Merced, San Joaquin, Solano, and Stanislaus—the fall in house prices led to a 50 percent drop in net worth. And all four counties were already below the median net worth in the United States in 2006. Prince Georges County, Maryland, just north of Washington, D.C., saw a 40 percent decline in net worth, and it was also well below the national median.

In 2000 the median household in Merced County, about 130 miles southeast of San Francisco, had an income of $35,000, which made it relatively poor compared to other areas of California. From 2002 to 2006, fueled by lending to households with low credit

scores, house prices in the county rose by 60 percent. Home owners responded by borrowing aggressively, and household debt increased by 80 percent. When the housing market turned sour, the
consequences were disastrous. Merced County saw a decline in
home equity of 50 percent from 2006 to 2009.

For many households during the Great Recession, the value of
their homes dropped below the amount still owed on the mortgage. Home owners then became "underwater" or "upside-down"
on their mortgage and actually had negative equity in their home.
If they chose to sell, they had to pay the difference between the
mortgage and the sale price to the bank. Faced with this dire cir-
cumstance, home owners could either stay in their homes and owe
the bank more than their homes were worth, or walk away and let
the bank foreclose.

Many chose to stay. In 2011, 11 million properties—23 percent of
all properties with a mortgage—had negative equity.[4] Even though
we know these numbers well, we are still shocked as we write them.
They are truly stunning and worth repeating: home owners in 1 out
of every 4 residential properties with a mortgage in the United
States were underwater. In the Central Valley counties mentioned
above, there were four zip codes with more than 70 percent of home
owners underwater. For Merced County, the number was 60 percent. Many other home owners walked away, allowing the bank to
foreclose. Walking away, of course, was not costless. Failing to pay a
mortgage payment shattered one's credit score. Further, foreclosures
led to a vicious cycle that further destroyed household net worth.

Foreclosures and Fire Sales

The negative effects of debt during the Great Recession extended
far beyond the indebted. When house prices collapsed, problems
related to excessive leverage infected the entire economy. The spill-
over effects included higher unemployment and a failing construction sector. But the most direct consequence was the startling rise
in foreclosures. Economists have long appreciated that debt affects

everyone when asset prices collapse. A fire sale of assets at steeply discounted prices is the most common reason why. A fire sale is a situation in which a debtor or creditor is willing to sell an asset for a price far below its market value. In the context of housing, this typically happens after a foreclosure: when a bank takes the property from a delinquent home owner, they sell it at a steeply discounted price.

After the sale, other home buyers and appraisers use the fire-sale price to estimate the prices of all other homes in the area. As a result, the prices of *all* the homes in the area suffer. Even home owners with no debt at all see the value of their homes decline. Consequently, financially healthy home owners may be unable to refinance their mortgages or sell their home at a fair price. Over the last few years, many home owners in the United States have been shocked by a very low appraisal of their home during a refinancing. This low appraisal was typically the direct result of an appraiser using a fire-sale foreclosure price to estimate the value of all homes in the neighborhood.

Some of the most insidious effects of debt financing are called the externalities of foreclosure. In the jargon of economists, a negative externality occurs whenever there are negative effects on other people from a private transaction between two parties. In a foreclosure, the bank selling the property does not bear the negative effects of a fire sale that all the other home owners in the area do. As a result, the bank is perfectly willing to sell at a lower price, even though society as a whole would not want the bank to do so.

Foreclosures greatly exacerbated the housing downturn during the Great Recession. In 2009 and 2010, foreclosures reached historically unprecedented levels. The last peak before the Great Recession was in 2001, when about 1.5 percent of all mortgages were in foreclosure. During the Great Recession, foreclosures were three times higher: about 5 percent of all mortgages were in foreclosure in 2009. Daniel Hartley has estimated that between 30 and 40 percent of all home sales in 2009 and 2010 were foreclosures or short sales.[5]

In research with Francesco Trebbi, we estimated some of the negative effects of foreclosures.[6] We used the fact that some states have more lenient foreclosure policies than others. In some states, for example, a lender must go through the courts to evict a delinquent borrower from a home. Other states require no court action, and, as one would expect, foreclosures are much faster in these states. As a result, there were far more foreclosures in some states than others during the Great Recession due to this fact alone, and this difference can be used to estimate the effects of foreclosures on local economies.

After following a similar trajectory from 2004 to 2006, house prices fell much more in states where foreclosure was easier. States that required a judicial foreclosure saw house prices fall 25 percent, whereas states not requiring judicial foreclosure saw house prices fall more than 40 percent. Figure 2.3 shows house prices over time in both types of states—the sharp relative decline in house prices in states not requiring a judicial foreclosure is clear.[7] Using this difference across states, our research concludes that house prices declined by 1.9 percentage points for every 1 percent of home owners going into foreclosure between 2007 and 2009. Further, by pulling down house prices, foreclosures dampened consumption and home building.

Debt-induced fire sales are not limited to the housing market. Andrei Shleifer and Robert Vishny emphasize the importance of fire sales following the leveraged-buyout wave of the late 1980s.[8] In that episode, companies with extremely high leverage were forced to sell assets at steeply discounted prices, which then lowered the value of collateral for all businesses. John Geanakoplos has written extensively on the impact of fire sales.[9] His work demonstrates how default means that an asset is transferred from someone for whom it's worth a lot (the borrower) to someone for whom it's worth much less (the lender). The lender does not want the property, and the borrower cannot afford it. As a result, the lender is forced to sell the asset at a depressed price. This leads to a vicious cycle. Defaults rise when asset prices collapse. But the rise in de-

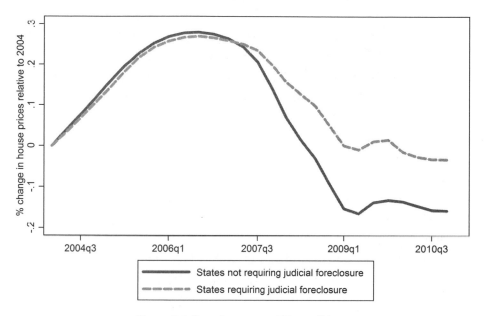

Figure 2.3: Foreclosures and House Prices

faults leads to depressed fire-sale prices as lenders unload the asset. This leads to even more defaults as even lower prices induce more borrowers to default.

When the housing bubble burst, there was undoubtedly a need for reallocation of resources in the economy. Too many renters had become home owners. Too many home owners had moved into homes they could not afford. Too many homes had been built. But when the crash occurred, the debt-ridden economy was unable to reallocate resources in an efficient manner. Instead, debt led to fire sales of properties, which only exacerbated the destruction of net worth.

Debt: The Anti-Insurance

There are about 350,000 residential fires in the United States every year.[10] If a family loses their house to a fire, the loss can be devastating. They will have to restart their lives from scratch, children may have to delay or completely give up on college, and certain medical needs may go unaddressed because the family can no longer afford such expenditures. Tornadoes and fires are examples of a number of such risks that we face every day. It makes no sense for individuals to bear these risks. Instead, a sound financial system should allow us to collectively insure one another against such risks that are beyond the control of any one person. It is a relatively small cost for us to protect each other on a regular basis, and the gains benefit everyone in the long run. When a family is able to move forward after a disaster, they can properly take care of their kids and can continue working. Our overall economic productivity and happiness are higher.

Debt is the anti-insurance. Instead of helping to share the risks associated with home ownership, it concentrates the risks on those least able to bear it. As we have shown, debt significantly amplified wealth inequality during the Great Recession. It also depressed prices through foreclosures. And once the decline in house prices destroyed the net worth of indebted home owners, one consequence proved disastrous—they stopped spending.

3: CUTTING BACK

A powerful narrative of the Great Recession focuses on the collapse of Lehman Brothers in September 2008. Allowing the bank to go bankrupt, the argument goes, was a "colossal error," and the failure to save it triggered the global economic downturn.[1] In an article on the causes of the Great Recession, Jacob Weisberg of the *Daily Beast* described it as "near-consensus" that "a global recession became inevitable once the government decided not to rescue Lehman Brothers."[2] This narrative is closely tied to the banking view articulated in chapter 1. According to this view, the collapse of Lehman Brothers froze the credit system, preventing businesses from getting the loans they needed to continue operating. As a result, they were forced to cut investment and lay off workers. In this narrative, if we could have prevented Lehman Brothers from failing, our economy would have remained intact.

The Consumption-Driven Recession

Is the collapse of Lehman Brothers the linchpin of any theory of the recession? Let's go back to the data. One of the facts that jumped out in chapter 1 is that the Great Recession was *consumption-driven*. Let's look more closely at the timing and magnitude of the spending declines.

The decline in spending was in full force *before* the fall of 2008. The National Bureau of Economic Research dates the beginning of the recession in the fourth quarter of 2007, three quarters before the failure of Lehman Brothers. The collapse in residential investment and durable consumption was dramatic well before the events of the fall of 2008. What happened in the fall of 2008 no doubt exacerbated economic weakness, but it should not be viewed as the primary cause.

Let's take a closer look at durable consumption and residential investment. Durable goods are those products that a consumer expects to last for a long time, like autos, furniture, appliances, and electronics. Residential investment reflects both new construction of housing units and remodeling of existing units. Both new construction and remodeling are a function of household demand for housing services. As a result, residential investment is best viewed as another form of household spending on durable goods.

The collapse in residential investment was already in full swing in 2006, a full two years before the collapse of Lehman Brothers. In the second quarter of 2006, residential investment fell by 17 percent on an annualized basis. In every quarter from the second quarter of 2006 through the second quarter of 2009, residential investment declined by at least 12 percent, reaching *negative* 30 percent in the fourth quarter of 2007 and the first quarter of 2008. The decline in residential investment alone knocked off 1.1 percent to 1.4 percent of GDP growth in the last three quarters of 2006.

While spending on other durable goods did not fall quite as early as residential investment, it still fell *before* the heart of the banking crisis. Compared to 2006, furniture purchases in 2007 were down 1.4 percent, and expenditures at home-improvement stores were down 4 percent. Spending on appliances was still up 2 percent in 2007, but the growth was significantly lower than the 7 percent growth in 2005 and 2006.

Looking within the year of 2008, however, provides important insights. The heart of the banking crisis began in September 2008, when both Lehman Brothers and AIG collapsed. So by focusing on January through August, we can estimate the pre-banking-crisis spending decline in 2008. As a benchmark, we want to compare spending in January through August 2008 to that in January through August 2007, because retail sales are seasonal. A clear pattern emerges. In 2008, auto spending was down 9 percent, furniture spending was down 8 percent, and home-improvement expenditures were down 5 percent. These declines were all registered *before* the collapse of Lehman Brothers. So the sharp reduction in household spending on durable goods had to have been triggered by something other than the banking crisis. The Monaco Coach Corporation example from chapter 1 is consistent with this evidence. Remember, large layoffs in the plants in northern Indiana occurred in the summer of 2008, before the peak of the banking crisis. Indeed, demand for motor homes collapsed in 2007 and early 2008, before Lehman Brothers failed.

Of course, the decline in overall household spending in the third and fourth quarters of 2008 *was* unprecedented. During these two quarters, overall consumption as measured by the National Income and Product Accounts (NIPA) declined by 5.2 percent. This was the largest two-quarter drop in NIPA-measured consumption in the historical data, which go back to 1947. The only other period that even comes close is that of the first and second quarters of 1980, when consumption fell by 4.6 percent. The collapse in consumption began before the end of 2008, but it no doubt accelerated during the banking crisis.

However, looking more closely at the banking-crisis period suggests that, even then, consumption was the key driver of the recession. NIPA breaks down the total output of the U.S. economy, or GDP, into its subcategories of consumption—investment, government spending, and net exports—and gives data on how much each contributes to overall GDP growth. We are particularly interested in the contributions of consumption and investment to GDP growth during the Great Recession. We split investment into residential investment and non-residential investment. The former reflects investment in housing services (both new construction and remodeling), while the latter reflects business investment in plants, capital goods, computers, and equipment.

Businesses and banks, as opposed to households, play the dominant role in the argument that troubles in the banking sector caused the recession. Under this argument, when Lehman Brothers collapsed, banks tightened credit, which forced businesses to massively cut non-residential investment and lay off workers. But the evidence from the NIPA accounts contradicts this argument. *Residential* investment was a serious drag on GDP growth even before the banking crisis. And the contribution of consumption was also negative in both the first and second quarters of 2008, which is consistent with the evidence above demonstrating that weakness in household spending preceded the banking crisis. In figure 3.1, we present this evidence for the Great Recession, which formally began in the fourth quarter of 2007. The figure splits out the contributions to total GDP growth from consumption, residential investment, and non-residential investment. As it illustrates, residential investment and consumption were the main drivers of weakness for the first three quarters of the recession.

But even more importantly, notice what happened during the worst part of the recession. In the third quarter of 2008, the collapse in GDP was driven by the collapse in *consumption*. Non-residential investment contributed negatively to GDP growth, but its effect was less than *half* the effect of consumption. Further, in the fourth quarter of 2008, consumption again registered the largest negative contribution to GDP growth. It wasn't until the first and second quarters of 2009 that business investment contributed most negatively to GDP growth.

The timing implicates household spending as the key driver of the recession, not the effects of the banking crisis on businesses. Job losses materialized because households stopped buying, not because businesses stopped investing. In fact, the evidence indicates that the decline in business investment was a *reaction* to the massive decline in household spending. If businesses saw no demand for their products, then of course they cut back on investment. To

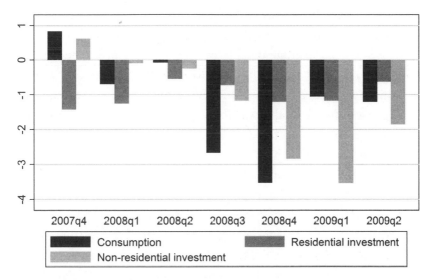

Figure 3.1: What Drove Recession? Contributions to GDP Growth

explain the decline in business investment at the end of 2008 and beginning of 2009, there is no need to rely on the banking crisis.

However, while the aggregate U.S. data demonstrate a clear pattern—consumption was the key driver of the recession—they alone do not perfectly distinguish the cause of the decline in spending. Perhaps the decline happened in anticipation of a banking crisis? Perhaps people somehow knew they were likely to be laid off in the future, so they cut back on durable purchases even before the recession began? Or perhaps the early decline in spending was driven by irrational fears? In the rest of this chapter, we use geographic data to explore the decline in household spending during the recession. These data allow us to see exactly where spending declined. As we will show, patterns emerge that help us make sense of why spending plummeted so dramatically.

Where Spending Declined[3]

We know from the previous chapter that some areas of the country were hit much harder by the housing collapse than others. Households in Florida, for example, faced an average decline of 16 percent in their net worth from the housing collapse, whereas households in Texas saw an average decline of only 2 percent. In the Central Valley of northern California, net worth collapsed by 50 percent. Examining data at a more specific level allows us to see whether the decline in housing wealth was the key driver of spending declines, as opposed to other factors like the collapse of Lehman Brothers. If the decline in net worth of indebted households was the key driver of the recession, we should expect household spending to fall much more steeply in areas that experienced the largest declines in housing net worth. And these drops should begin early in the recession.

We split counties in the United States into five quintiles based on the decline in net worth from 2006 to 2009 due to the collapse in house prices. Each quintile contains 20 percent of the total U.S. population. We call the quintile with the largest decline in net worth "large net-worth-decline counties," and we call the quintile with the smallest decline in net worth "small net-worth-decline counties." Large net-worth-decline counties were located in many states, including California, Florida, Georgia, Maryland, Michigan, and Virginia. Small net-worth-decline counties were also widespread across the country.

Large net-worth-decline counties lost an average of 26 percent of net worth, while small net-worth-decline counties lost almost exactly 0 percent. Recall that the decline in net worth coming from the housing crash can be decomposed into two factors: the decline in house prices and the leverage multiplier. As a result, areas of the country with higher debt burdens experienced a much larger percentage decline in net worth even for the same percentage decline in house prices. Large net-worth-decline counties were not just counties where house prices collapsed. Instead, they were counties that had a *combination* of high debt levels and a collapse in house prices.

From 2006 to 2009, large net-worth-decline counties cut back on consumption by almost 20 percent. This was massive. To put it into perspective, the total decline in spending for the U.S. economy

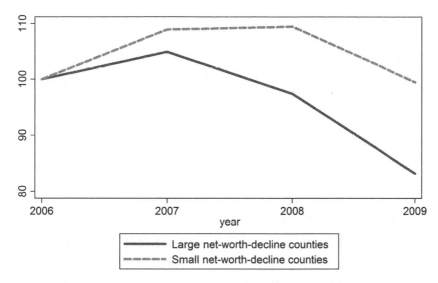

Figure 3.2: Spending in Large and Small Net-Worth Decline Counties

was about 5 percent during these same years. The decline in spending in these counties was four times the aggregate decline. In contrast, small net-worth-decline counties spent almost the exact same amount in 2006 as in 2009. Figure 3.2 shows spending in large and small net-worth-decline counties. (Both series are indexed to 2006.) Even as early as 2007, a large gap opened up between spending by counties with large and small declines in net worth. Clear signs of the recession emerged very early in counties hit with a negative net-worth shock. But 2008 was the year in which the difference accelerated substantially. In fact, in counties with only a small decline in home-equity values, household spending actually *rose* from 2007 to 2008. If we examine only U.S. counties that avoided the collapse in net worth through 2008, we wouldn't even see much evidence of a recession. In contrast, spending in areas with a large decline in net worth collapsed in 2008.

Of course, the effects of the economic disaster were ultimately felt even in areas that avoided the collapse in net worth. After rising from 2006 to 2008, spending in 2009 fell by almost 10 percent in counties with the smallest decline in net worth. But the decline in these counties in 2009 doesn't invalidate the importance of the shock to net worth. When spending fell in large net-worth-decline counties, the damage was not limited. It spread throughout the entire country. (We return to this point in chapter 5 when we discuss unemployment during the Great Recession.)

The tremendous effect of net-worth declines on spending can be seen very clearly by zeroing in on the colossal housing mess in the Central Valley in California. As mentioned earlier, four counties with steep drops in house prices—Merced, San Joaquin, Solano, and Stanislaus—witnessed a decline in net worth of about 50 percent. The spending response was dramatic, as spending in these counties fell by 30 percent from 2006 to 2009. Much of this occurred very early in the recession. Compared to the summer of 2006, auto purchases in the summer of 2008—before the collapse of Lehman Brothers—were already down 35 percent. The banking crisis in the fall of 2008 cannot explain why spending had already fallen so steeply in the Central Valley in the summer of 2008.

The geographic pattern is sharp. Areas of the country suffering a collapse in net worth pulled back much earlier and much more strongly than areas that didn't. We attribute this to the decreased net worth of indebted households. But even if one believes other channels were more important, the pattern in figure 3.2 dampens alternative hypotheses. Whatever one wants to blame for the severe recession, it must be consistent with the strong geographic pattern in the spending data.

What's Debt Got to Do with It?

In November 2011, James Surowiecki wrote an article titled "The Deleveraging Myth" in his influential *New Yorker* column, in which he claimed that debt was not the main reason household spending had collapsed during the Great Recession. Instead, he argued that the decline in house prices alone, even in the absence of debt, easily explained weakness in consumer spending. As he put it, "It's well established that when housing prices go up people feel richer and spend more. . . . But when housing prices go down people cut their spending by the same amount in response. That means that—even if consumers had no debt at all—we'd expect a dropoff in consumption."[4]

This argument is a common one that we have heard when presenting our research: a housing-wealth effect alone, even in a world without debt, can explain why household spending declined by so much when house prices collapsed. However, in our view, there are two problems with this argument. First, recall the foreclosure externality we described in the previous chapter. Foreclosures have a dramatic effect on house prices. In the absence of debt, there would have been no foreclosures, and house prices would not have fallen as much as they did. We will quantify the effect of foreclosures on spending later in the book, but the important point is that we cannot treat the decline in house prices as independent of debt.

Second, in the pure housing-wealth-effect view, the distribution of net worth is unimportant. The collapse in house prices would be disastrous for household spending regardless of which households bear the loss. As we outlined in the previous chapter, debt concentrates the losses on those with the least net worth. This begs the question: Does the fact that debt forces losses on the lowest net-worth borrowers amplify the effect of house-price declines on spending? In the pure housing-wealth-effect view, it does not. In the debt-centric view, it does.

Let's look at the data. The geographic patterns in spending show that the negative shock to net worth caused people to spend less. In economic jargon, the spending response is called the marginal propensity to consume, or the MPC, out of housing wealth. The MPC out of housing wealth tells us how many dollars less an individual spends in response to a wealth shock. For example, if an individual responds to a $10,000 fall in home value by cutting spending by $500, then the MPC is ($500/$10,000 =) $0.05 per $1. The larger the MPC, the more responsive the household is to the same change in wealth. In the pure housing-wealth-effect view, everyone has the same MPC and hence debt does not matter.

Our research estimates an MPC out of housing wealth during the recession on the order of 5 to 7 cents per dollar. In other words, if an individual's house price fell by $10,000 during the Great Recession, the individual cut spending on average about $500 to $700. Given the aggregate decline in home values of about $5.5 trillion, our estimate implies that the decline in home values led to a $275 to $385 billion decline in retail spending, which is a very large amount.

But this estimate is only the *average* MPC across the entire population. It does not tell us who cut back the most. If debt matters for spending over and above the pure housing-wealth effect, we should expect a *higher* MPC out of housing wealth for indebted households. Or, in other words, a household with more debt would respond to the same decline in house prices by cutting back more aggressively on spending.

This is a crucial point, so here is a simple example to clarify. Two households live next door to each other. They had identical homes in 2006, both worth $100,000. Household D (for Debt) had an $80,000 mortgage, which they borrowed from household N (for No debt), and household N had no mortgage at all. So in 2006, household D had a home equity of $20,000 and a leverage ratio of 80 percent. Household N had a home equity of $100,000, a leverage ratio of 0 percent, and a financial asset (the mortgage) worth $80,000.

From 2006 to 2009, house prices in their neighborhood fell 10 percent, or $10,000. So in 2009, both Household D and N had a home worth $90,000 instead of $100,000. Both lost $10,000 of home equity from 2006 to 2009. The mortgage of Household D remained worth $80,000. Household N owns the mortgage, but there is no change in its value. Therefore, both households saw a total drop in their wealth of $10,000 driven completely by the change in home equity. Household D has remaining net worth of $10,000, whereas Household N has remaining net worth of $170,000, comprised of $90,000 of home equity and the $80,000 mortgage asset.

The key question is: Which household cut spending by more? Both lost $10,000. If the decline in spending is just a housing-wealth effect, then debt is irrelevant for understanding how much home owners cut spending in response to a decline in wealth. In our example, this translates to saying that both household D and N had the same MPC out of housing wealth. In this view, if both households have the same MPC of 0.05, then both households cut spending by $500. If these two households have the same MPC, then debt indeed does not matter. Only the decline in home values is relevant.

But what should we expect if debt does matter? If debt amplifies the effect of house-price declines on spending, we would expect to see a higher MPC for household D than household N. In other words, the indebted household pulls back on spending more for the exact same decline in home value. If household D has a higher MPC than household N, then the distribution of leverage matters when house prices collapse. If the house-price decline concentrates losses on the people with the most debt, then the effects on their consumption will be especially severe.

The MPC of households is also relevant for thinking about the effectiveness of government stimulus programs for boosting demand. When the government sends out stimulus checks to spur consumer demand, as it did in both 2001 and 2008, policy makers want to understand how much of the stimulus check will be spent. The policy will be considered more effective if individuals spend a larger share of the checks, which would happen if individuals who get the checks have higher MPCs.

More than a Wealth Effect

Our research directly tests if the MPC varies by household income and leverage by focusing on zip-code-level information on auto purchases. Zip-code-level data lets us go inside counties that saw large net-worth shocks and see if they cut spending the most during the Great Recession. More specifically, our research estimates how much a household with high leverage versus low leverage cut spending on autos in response to the same dollar value decline in house prices. In other words, our research estimates how the MPC out of housing wealth varies with household leverage during the Great Recession.

The results are dramatic and strongly indicate that Household D in the example above would cut back far more than Household N. In the real world, a household with a loan-to-value ratio of 90 percent or higher in their home in 2006 had an MPC out of housing wealth that was more than three times as large as a household with a loan-to-value ratio of 30 percent or lower. For example, in response to a $10,000 decline in home value, households with an LTV higher than 90 percent cut spending on autos by $300. Households with an LTV lower than 30 percent cut spending on autos by less than $100. For the exact same dollar decline in home value, households with more debt cut back on spending more aggressively. Figure 3.3 shows the MPC estimates across the distribution of leverage. There is a strong relation: the higher the leverage in the home, the more aggressively the household cuts back on spending when home values decline.

The higher MPC out of housing wealth for highly levered households is one of the most important results from our research. It immediately implies that the distribution of wealth and debt matters. During the Great Recession, house-price declines weren't the same for households with high leverage versus those with low leverage— they fell the most for households that had the highest leverage. As we discussed in the last chapter, these were households with low net worth and all of their wealth tied to home equity. As a result, the collapse of the housing market was especially toxic for them. Not only did house prices fall, but they fell most for households with the highest MPC out of housing wealth. Put another way, the decline in spending from 2006 to 2009 would have been far less severe if house prices fell more for households with low debt levels and a large amount of financial assets.[5]

The MPC differences across the population can also help us understand other spectacular asset-price collapses, like the bursting of the dot-com bubble in the early 2000s. We shouldn't for-

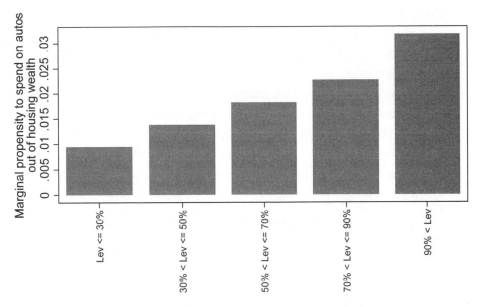

Figure 3.3: MPC Based on Housing Leverage Ratio

get that this represented a huge loss in wealth. From 2000 to 2002, households in the United States lost $5 trillion in financial asset value, mostly from the decline in stocks. This is remarkably similar to lost housing wealth during the Great Recession. Yet despite this dramatic decline in financial wealth during the tech bust, household spending barely budged. In fact, household spending *grew* from 2000 to 2002 by 5 percent. This was lower than the 15 percent growth in household spending from 1998 to 2000, but it was nowhere near the *decline* in spending of 8 percent from 2007 to 2009.

So the bursting of the tech bubble resulted in a huge loss of household wealth but had little effect on household spending, while the bursting of the housing bubble during the Great Recession had a great effect. Why? The differential MPCs shown above provide the answer: tech stocks were owned by very rich households with almost no leverage. As of 2001, almost 90 percent of all stocks in the United States were owned by the top 20 percent of the net-worth distribution. And these households had a leverage ratio of only 6 percent (that is, these households had only $6 of debt for every $100 of assets). Rich households with little debt tend to have a very low MPC out of wealth. As a result, we shouldn't be surprised that the bursting of the tech bubble had almost no impact on spending.

A comparison of the tech-bubble and housing-bubble collapses offers a useful lesson as we move forward. Asset-price declines are never a good thing. But they are extremely dangerous when the asset is highly levered. The combination of high debt levels and a sharp asset-price decline results in a massive decline in spending.

A Summary of the Evidence

We started this book with a challenging puzzle: economic contractions lead to painful job losses, but we don't understand exactly why. Solving any mystery requires a collection of facts. We have now shown a number of facts that help uncover the mechanism leading to these economic catastrophes. In the next chapter, we will outline the exact theory that we believe explains why severe recessions happen. But first, we want to summarize the evidence so far presented.

The initial piece of evidence is that severe economic downturns are almost always preceded by a sharp run-up in household debt. This was true of the Great Recession and the Great Depression in the United States. It was also true of many of the worst economic contractions in Europe in the last decade. Even back in 1994, scholars recognized the strong relation between the severity of recessions and the increase in household debt that preceded them. Further, recessions are triggered when household spending collapses.

Another important fact is how debt distributes losses when asset prices like home values collapse. During the Great Recession in the United States, the housing bust disproportionately affected low net-worth, highly indebted home owners. Indebted home owners bore the first losses associated with the collapse in house prices; as a result, they saw a massive collapse in their net worth. The financial system's reliance on debt means that those with the most wealth were protected when house prices fell, while those with the least were hammered. Wealth inequality, which was already severe before the Great Recession, increased substantially from 2006 to 2009.

When one sees the geography of spending patterns, the mysterious collapse in consumption during the Great Recession isn't so mysterious. Counties with high household-debt burdens and a large decline in house prices cut back sharply on spending when home-owner net worth was decimated. Counties that avoided the collapse in net worth saw almost no decline in spending even through 2008. Eventually, however, even counties that avoided the collapse in housing saw a decline in spending.

Finally, debt is critical to understanding the collapse in consumption. It amplifies the loss in home values due to the foreclosure externality, and it concentrates losses on the indebted households that have the highest marginal propensity to consume.

As we mentioned at the beginning of this book, people like those laid off in northern Indiana deserve an evidence-based explanation for why they lost their jobs during the Great Recession. We now have a collection of facts that brings us closer to providing such an explanation. In the following chapters, we propose a theory of economic contractions that can explain why debt leads to severe economic contractions, and why millions of jobs are lost as a result.

4: LEVERED LOSSES: THE THEORY

Hal Varian, the chief economist at Google and a professor emeritus of economics at the University of California, Berkeley, believes in the power of data. "Between the dawn of civilization and 2003," he said in a recent interview, "we only created five exabytes of information; now we're creating that amount every two days." He has famously pronounced that "the sexy job in the next 10 years will be statisticians." Varian also understands that the explosion of data requires increased skill in interpreting them. As he put it, "The ability to take data—to be able to understand it, to process it, to extract value from it, to visualize it, to communicate it—that's going to be a hugely important skill in the next decades."[1] As you've probably guessed, we share Varian's passion for data, which is why we've spent the last three chapters collecting facts to help us understand the cause of severe economic downturns. But we also agree with Varian's message on the skills required to *interpret* data correctly.

The ability to interpret data is especially important in macroeconomics. The aggregate U.S. economy is an unwieldy object—it contains millions of firms and households. Their interactions with each other are like an ecosystem where one party's actions affect everyone else. With the information explosion described by Varian, one could collect an infinite number of data points to figure out what is going on. What actions are driving the economy? Whose behavior is most important? What actions could help resuscitate economic activity? But unless an economist can put some structure on the data, he or she will drown in a deep ocean of numbers trying to answer these questions.

Which brings us to the importance of an economic model. Macroeconomists are defined in large part by the theoretical model they use to approach the data. A model provides the structure needed to see which data are most important, and to decide on the right course of action given the information that is available. This chapter presents the core economic model in this book, a model we refer to as the *levered-losses* framework. It is motivated by the facts we have uncovered so far. We need a model that rationalizes why recessions are preceded by a large rise in household debt and why they begin with a dramatic decline in spending. The theory we present connects these dots to explain why a collapse in asset prices when an economy has elevated debt levels leads to economic disaster with massive job losses.

In our explanation of the levered-losses framework, we start with the standard benchmark frictionless macroeconomic model, which we have referred to before as the *fundamentals* view.[2] We view this model as unrealistic and unable to explain severe economic contractions. But it is nonetheless important to understand before delving into the levered-losses framework. Only by understanding the fundamentals view can we appreciate the departures from it that cause economic disasters.

The Fundamentals View and Robinson Crusoe

The basic idea behind the fundamentals view is that the total output, or GDP, of the economy is determined by its productive capacity: workers, capital, and the technology of firms. The economy is defined by what it can produce, not by what is demanded. Total production is limited only by natural barriers, like the rate at which our machines can convert various inputs into output, the number of working hours in a day per person, and the willingness of people to work versus relax. This is sometimes called the *supply-side* view because it emphasizes the productive capacity, or supply, of resources.

Given the emphasis on the supply side of the economy, economic fluctuations in these models are driven by changes in the economy's productive capacity. For example, one of the crucial building blocks of the fundamentals view is the "Robinson Crusoe" economy, which is an economy with just one person, Robinson Crusoe, and one good, coconuts.[3] The production of coconuts is determined by the number of coconut trees ("capital") and the amount Robinson Crusoe chooses to work to get the coconuts from the trees ("labor supply"). The GDP of this economy is the total number of coconuts produced given capital and labor supply.

What causes a severe contraction in output in this simplified economy? Any shock to the island that destroys productive capacity. A hurricane is an obvious example. If a hurricane hits the island and destroys a large number of coconut trees, then the production of coconuts falls considerably. The economy goes through a "recession" characterized by lower coconut consumption, where the decline in consumption is driven by the hurricane's destruction of productive capacity. The output of the economy is determined by the available resources for production, not by any shift in demand.

Further, unless productive capacity is diminished, it is very difficult to understand why Robinson Crusoe would all of a sudden choose to massively cut coconut consumption. In the absence of some disastrous event, the only reason Robinson would cut coconut consumption would be a change in his preferences or beliefs. For example, perhaps he wakes up one morning and decides he would prefer to delay eating coconuts until later in life. Or perhaps he has a belief that a hurricane is coming, so he needs to save up on coconuts. These kinds of shocks are difficult to measure and, in our view, hard to justify in practice.

The fundamentals view has a difficult time explaining severe contractions in advanced economies. Severe contractions are almost never associated with an obvious shock to the productive capacity of the economy. For example, no severe calamity such as war or natural disaster initiated the Great Depression, the Great Recession, or the current economic malaise plaguing Europe. There was no loss of technological capacity. We did not forget how to make cars, airplanes, or houses. And while the price of real estate crashed during each of these episodes, we did not witness a destruction of homes or buildings. *Severe recessions are triggered even when no obvious destruction of productive capacity occurs.*

The failure of the fundamentals view can be boiled down to two main issues. First, severe recessions are not initiated by some calamity that destroys the productive capacity of the economy. They are set off when asset prices collapse and households sharply pull back on spending. Second, in the fundamentals view, even if we have some shock that causes a decline in spending, there is no obvious reason why the economy would suffer. That is, lower spending in the fundamentals view does not lead to contraction or job loss. Remember, output in the fundamentals view is determined by the *productive capacity* of the economy, not by *demand*. In response to a sharp decline in consumption, the economy in the fundamentals view has natural corrective forces that keep it operating at full capacity. These include lower interest rates and consumer prices, which we explain further below. Obviously, however, these corrective forces weren't able to keep the economy on track.

Significant departures from the fundamentals view are needed to explain severe contractions, and any theory that departs from the fundamentals view must address these key issues. An alternative theory must explain why households sharply pull back on spending, and why the cut in spending is so destructive for total output. Why doesn't the economy adjust to lower spending? Why does economic output decline? Why do people lose their jobs? The levered-losses framework answers these questions and is strongly supported by the data. Let's go through it.

The Levered-Losses Framework[4]

The first ingredient of the levered-losses framework is differences across the population due to debt. There are borrowers and savers in the economy, and the borrowers have substantial leverage. They borrow in the form of debt contracts from savers, and these debt contracts require an interest payment each period. The debt contract gives the saver the *senior claim* on the assets of the borrower. Or, in other words, in the event that the borrower does not pay, the saver has the right to foreclose on the assets of the borrower. If the house price falls and the borrower sells, he must still pay back the full amount of the mortgage. The borrower has the junior claim on the home and therefore experiences the first losses associated with any decline in house prices.

Borrowers tend to be households that have low net worth, which is exactly the reason they have to borrow to buy a home. Savers tend to be households that have high net worth. In the model, the savers lend directly to the borrowers, which is equivalent to saying the rich lend to the poor. In reality, of course, the savers put their money into a bank, a money-market fund, or direct holdings of financial assets such as stocks. That money finds its way into mortgages for the borrower. The point remains: Savers, through their financial holdings, have the senior claim on the underlying houses. The rich are protected against house-price declines not only because they are rich but also because they have a senior claim on housing.

The second ingredient of the levered-losses framework is a shock to the economy that leads to a sharp pullback in spending by debt-burdened families. This shock can be viewed generally as any event that lowers the net-worth position of levered households or makes it more difficult for them to borrow. Practically speaking, a collapse in real estate prices is almost always the shock. As we showed in chapter 2, the collapse in house prices during the Great Recession destroyed the net worth of indebted households.

The spending impact of the fall in real estate prices is *amplified* in the levered-losses framework due to two effects. The first is the concentration of losses on those who have the highest spending sensitivity with respect to housing wealth: debtors. The second is the amplification of the original house-price shock due to foreclosures.

When debt concentrates losses on indebted households, there are several reasons why they stop spending. One is that they must rebuild their wealth in order to make sure they have money to spend in the future. For example, consider a married couple in their late fifties approaching retirement. They had 20 percent equity in their home that they were planning on using to finance their retirement, either by downsizing and selling their home, or by taking out a home-equity loan. When house prices collapse by 20 percent and their home equity disappears, they are in dire straits. They no longer have sufficient wealth to cover their planned spending in retirement. As a result, they cut spending in order to build up savings.[5]

Beyond the immediate effect of wanting to save more due to lost wealth, levered households also cut back on spending due to tighter constraints on borrowing. For example, levered households no longer have sufficient home equity to use as collateral for borrowing. They are also likely to have a hard time refinancing into a lower mortgage interest rate. These tighter borrowing constraints depress spending by indebted households. The overall decline in spending in the levered-losses framework is larger than it would be if the housing losses were more *equally distributed* across the population. As we have demonstrated in chapter 3, the spending of indebted households is more sensitive to housing-wealth losses than the spending of savers. In other words, savers can absorb losses much more easily without reducing their spending.

The second channel through which debt amplifies the impact of housing shock is the foreclosure externality discussed in chapter 2. If the initial decline in house prices is large enough, some of the indebted home owners may owe more on their house than it is worth. Underwater households are much more likely to default on their mortgage payments, either because the payment becomes prohibitively expensive or because of strategic motives. Regardless, these defaults lead to foreclosures that in turn lead to further reductions in house prices. Spending cuts driven by the initial decline in home values are further amplified as foreclosures push house prices further down.

While we have focused on the example of creditor and debtor households in our levered-losses framework, the intuition applies more broadly. For example, the borrower may be a country, such as Spain, that has borrowed substantially from another country, such as Germany. A fall in house prices in Spain in this example forces Spanish households to cut back sharply on spending for the same reasons discussed above. Germany is protected from the house-price declines because Germans have the senior claim on the Spanish housing stock.

We have now described how a large decline in spending occurs in the levered-losses framework, a decline that the fundamentals view cannot easily explain. But as we pointed out above, there is an additional failure of the fundamentals view we must address. In the fundamentals view, the economy has natural corrective forces that keep it operating at full capacity, even if there is a severe decline in spending.

How Does the Economy Try to React?

The first way that the economy tries to prevent economic catastrophe when indebted households cut back is through a sharp reduction in interest rates. As borrowers rebuild their balance sheets by reducing borrowing, the demand for savings in the economy rises. This pushes interest rates down as money flows into the financial system where nobody is borrowing. Eventually, interest rates should become low enough to induce businesses to borrow and invest, which should help make up for lower consumer spending. Further, savers in the economy, those less affected by the decline in house prices, should be induced to spend more—extremely low interest rates should encourage savers to buy a new car or remodel their kitchen. This process is aided by the central bank, which typically responds to a crisis by pushing down short-term interest rates. Spending by savers and investment by businesses should fill in for the gap left by borrowers cutting back, and the aggregate economy should escape unharmed.

The economy also tries to prevent economic catastrophe through the goods market: when spending collapses, businesses reduce prices. As prices decline, buyers should eventually return to the market. Similarly, for a smaller country that relies heavily on exports, a decline in domestic spending will lead to exchange-rate depreciation, which makes that country's exports less expensive to foreigners and should boost domestic output. All together, the combination of lower interest rates, lower domestic prices, and a depreciated currency is how an economy tries to handle a massive negative demand shock from indebted households.

But we already know that these adjustments don't work. In the Great Recession, the economy was unable to react to the massive demand shock from indebted households. There must be *frictions* that prevent these adjustments—frictions that amplify the decline in spending by levered households into a nationwide recession with high unemployment.

The Frictions

The most well-known friction is called the zero lower bound on nominal interest rates.[6] The zero lower bound means that interest rates cannot get low enough to actually induce savers in the economy to start buying. If interest rates cannot decrease enough, the gap in spending left by levered households cutting back remains unfilled. This is also referred to as the "liquidity trap," because when an interest rate is kept at zero when it needs to be negative, people save their money in liquid instruments such as cash and U.S. government treasury bills. Instead of spending, savers hoard money in risk-free assets.

The zero lower bound on interest rates exists because the government issues paper money—cash—which cannot have a negative return.[7] We normally value cash for its transaction purposes: paying the babysitter or the parking valet at a restaurant. But cash is also an asset. You could theoretically hold all of your assets in cash. If you put all of your money into cash, what is the worst interest rate you could possibly get? The answer: 0 percent. In the absence of inflation, cash will always yield an interest rate of 0 percent for the investor, and it is risk-free. Given that any investor could always hold a risk-free asset (cash) and be guaranteed a return of 0 percent, no asset can ever have a negative expected nominal return. This means there is a *zero lower bound* on interest rates: no nominal interest rate in the economy can be below 0 percent.

Suppose instead savers were *charged* for saving money in the bank. If you put $100 in today, you get only $90 out in a year. In such a situation, the saver would be induced to buy goods instead of save—why let money rot in the bank when you could buy a new home or car? Savers would consume in response to negative interest rates, therefore helping to offset the decline in spending by borrowers.

But the zero lower bound on interest rates prevents interest rates from becoming negative. In the example above, if a bank tried to charge you $10 for putting money in a deposit account, you would take the money and put it in your safe at home, which would guarantee you a 0 percent return—hence, the zero lower bound. As a result, the economy is stuck in a liquidity trap. Borrowers cannot spend as they rebuild their balance sheets and face severe borrowing constraints. Savers refuse to spend because interest rates are not sufficiently *negative* to induce them to consume.[8] Economic activity then becomes *demand-driven*. Anything that can induce households in the economy to spend will increase total output. It should come as no surprise that almost every major economic contraction in history is associated with very low nominal interest rates. As we write, interest rates on short-term U.S. treasury bills have been 0 percent for five years.

Inflation is an obvious way of getting real interest rates into negative territory. Inflation acts similarly to a bank charging a saver for holding cash. For now, we will ignore inflation (but will return to it in the policy section of the book in chapter 11).

What about lower consumer prices? Shouldn't they make people want to spend? The answer again is no, and a decline in consumer prices may even make the problem worse. Lower prices are possible only if firms lower their costs—by reducing wages. However, a wage cut crushes indebted households who have debt burdens fixed in nominal terms. If an indebted household faces a wage cut while their mortgage payment remains the same, they are likely to cut spending even further. This leads to a vicious cycle in which indebted households cut spending, which leads firms to reduce wages, which leads to higher debt burdens for households, which leads them to cut back even further. This was famously dubbed the "debt-deflation" cycle by Irving Fisher in the aftermath of the Great Depression.[9]

There are several other important frictions that prevent the economy from adjusting to a severe spending shock. For example, borrowers tend to buy different types of products than savers. If borrowers start buying less, the economy would need to ramp down production of goods that borrowers like and ramp up production of goods that savers like. There are frictions in the reallocation process. The economy may need to transfer workers from the construction sector to other sectors. It may need to transfer workers from local retail to industries exporting to other countries in an effort to boost output via depreciation.[10] It may need to transfer spending from borrowers to savers. Generally, any friction that prevents such reallocation will translate the decline in spending by levered households into a severe economic recession with high unemployment.

We Are in This Together

When debtors sharply pull back on household spending, frictions such as the zero lower bound prevent savers from making up for the shortfall. But the disastrous economic effects of lower demand are not borne uniquely by debtors—they spread through the entire economy. Levered losses affect even those who never had any debt during the boom.

The most devastating knock-on effect of lower demand driven by levered losses is a massive increase in unemployment. Even workers living in areas completely immune from the housing bust lose their jobs because of the decline in household spending. The Monaco Coach Corporation is a useful example. Northern Indiana didn't have high debt levels or even a large collapse in house prices. Why did these workers lose their jobs?

Tackling the reasons for high unemployment is a serious challenge. Even today, macroeconomists continue a long and heated debate on the reasons for and even the existence of involuntary unemployment. Standard macroeconomic models struggle with involuntary unemployment because wages should adjust to shocks in order to equate the amount that households want to work ("labor supply") with the amount that firms want to hire ("labor demand"). Involuntary unemployment can only exist in a macroeconomic model if there are some "rigidities" that prevent wages from adjusting and workers from finding jobs.

We'll start with a simple example to illustrate employment dynamics in the face of levered losses.[11] Suppose an economy is made up of two islands, Debtor Island and Creditor Island. Everyone on Debtor Island has very large debt burdens, whereas no one on Creditor Island has any debt. Households on both Debtor Island and Creditor Island consume two goods: autos and haircuts. Autos can be traded between Debtor Island and Creditor Island, whereas haircuts cannot. In other words, employment in the auto industry on each island is a function of total demand on both Debtor and Creditor Islands, whereas employment in barbershops depends only on the number of haircuts demanded on the local island. We assume that people cannot move across the islands; they are stuck where they are.

Let's suppose that house prices collapse on Debtor Island. Levered losses lead to a sharp pullback in spending on cars and haircuts on that island. If wages and prices flexibly adjust, what should we expect to happen? Demand for haircuts comes only from those living on Debtor Island; as a result, lower demand for haircuts will push down the price of haircuts. This will in turn push down the wage of barbers on Debtor Island. Barbers don't like lower wages, so many barbers will quit to go work in the auto industry.

But more workers in the auto industry will also push down wages at the auto plant until the wages in the auto plant and the barbershop are equalized. Auto manufacturers will have more available workers, so they will pay them less. For Debtor Island, the end result will be higher employment in the auto industry, fewer barbers, and lower wages. But total employment will not change. Workers will move out of barbershops and into the auto industry, and they will be forced to accept lower wages.

Creditor Island is connected to Debtor Island through the auto industry. So even though Creditor Island has not experienced levered losses, it will nonetheless be affected. Wages fell on Debtor Island in the auto industry, which allows auto manufacturers on Debtor Island to sell cars more cheaply. Because autos produced on Debtor Island can be sold on Creditor Island, Creditor Island manufacturers must respond by also lowering auto prices—and the wages paid to autoworkers. On Creditor Island, autoworkers respond to lower wages by leaving the auto plant to become barbers. But of course, this pushes down the wage of barbers until it is again equalized with the lower wage in the auto plant. Even in this example in which wages and prices flexibly adjust, Creditor Island households are directly affected by levered losses on Debtor Island. They must now accept lower wages.

But much more severe problems exist if wages and prices do not fully adjust. Let's suppose we have full price and wage rigidity, so neither prices nor wages adjust in the face of lower demand from Debtor Island households. When house prices collapse on Debtor

Island, households again cut spending on autos and haircuts. Auto plants and barbershops will bring in less revenue, and they will need to cut costs. But if they cannot lower wages in response to this decline in demand, both auto plants and barbershops will be forced to lay off workers. Debtor Island experiences a sharp increase in unemployment.

But here is the crucial insight: *Creditor Island also suffers high unemployment.* When Debtor Island households cut back on auto spending, Creditor Island auto plants have lower demand for their cars from Debtor Island, and therefore lower revenue. If they cannot lower costs by lowering wages, they will fire workers. Fired autoworkers will try to get hired at the barbershop, but the inability of wages to decline will prevent them from getting a job. As a result, workers on Creditor Island become unemployed even though they never had any debt at all.

This simple example assumes wage rigidity to prevent the reallocation needed to maintain full employment. Debtor Island workers need to switch from barbershops to the auto industry, and Creditor Island workers need to switch from the auto industry to barbershops. When a local economy suffers a demand shock, workers need to be reallocated from sectors catering to local demand to sectors catering to external demand. Flexible wages would allow this reallocation to occur, while rigid wages prevent it. But of course, there are many other frictions that would serve the same role. In this example, if barbers need extensive training to become autoworkers and vice versa, we would also see a rise in unemployment when the demand shock occurred.

We do not mean to give the impression that flexible wages are the solution. We have already seen how a reduction in wages for indebted households exacerbates the spending problem due to what Irving Fisher calls the "debt-deflation" cycle. The bottom line is that very serious adjustments in the economy are required when levered households cut spending. Wages need to fall, and workers need to switch into new industries. Frictions in this reallocation process translate the spending decline into large job losses.

Reallocation?

A common argument put forward during the contraction is that we should rely on the reallocation process to save us from disaster. Allow wages to fall and workers to reallocate, the argument goes. But this approach faces enormous obstacles. The economy requires quick adjustment in response to such a massive decline in spending. Any friction that prevents quick adjustment will hurt the entire economy. A more effective approach would prevent the sharp decline in spending by targeting the levered-losses problem directly. This will be a major theme of our policy recommendations later in the book.

The important lesson from this example is that we are in this mess together. Even households in the economy that stayed away from toxic debt during the boom suffer the consequences of the collapse in household spending during the bust. For example, many auto plants in the United States are in areas of the country that completely avoided the housing boom and bust: Indiana, Ohio, and Kentucky. Yet autoworkers in these states suffered during the Great Recession because highly levered households in other parts of the country stopped buying cars. Employment is the most important channel through which levered losses propagates through the economy. But there are also other channels. When highly levered households default on their obligations, foreclosures by banks depress house prices throughout the neighborhood. Defaults also lead banks to cut back on lending to other households. The entire country suffers.

In an economic crisis brought about by levered losses, the natural reactions are moral judgment and outrage. A common refrain we hear is that irresponsible home owners borrowed too much, and they should be made to suffer. But such moralizing during the crisis is also counterproductive. The problem of levered losses quickly spreads throughout the economy; the sharp pullback in household spending by levered households affects us all.

5: EXPLAINING UNEMPLOYMENT

In January 2012 Senator Bob Corker, a Republican from Tennessee, blasted the Obama administration's proposal to write down principal on underwater home mortgages at taxpayer expense. He called it "terrible public policy." His office released a harsh statement: "[The legislation] means Tennesseans and other Americans who acted responsibly will be paying for the consequences of reckless housing practices in other states like California, Florida, Nevada, and New York, where exotic mortgages and no down payment loans were most prevalent prior to the 2008 financial crisis." To prevent such bailouts for reckless home owners, Senator Corker said, "I intend to introduce a bill this week that says if states like California or Florida want to reduce principal on mortgages in their states, they can do so themselves with state money, not with federal taxpayer dollars."[1]

From the perspective of his constituents in Tennessee, would helping home owners in hard-hit housing states indeed be "terrible public policy," as Senator Corker argued? Let's examine the Tennessean economy a bit closer to answer this question. Senator Corker was correct that Tennessee mostly avoided the housing boom and bust. From 2002 to 2006, house prices in Tennessee rose by only 25 percent, far below the 60 percent growth in California and Florida. Households in Tennessee came into the recession with debt levels well below the national average, and net worth dropped by only 2 percent during the housing crash.

So Tennessee avoided the housing boom and crash, but does that mean they were immune to the disaster in other states? Would Tennesseans be better off forcing hard-hit households in California and Florida to fend for themselves? The problem with Senator Corker's logic is that Tennessee is not an isolated island. Jobs in Tennessee are highly dependent on the performance of the rest of the U.S. economy. For example, Tennessee had a thriving auto manufacturing industry in 2007. In fact, Tennessee had the sixth highest fraction of workers in the auto manufacturing industry of any state in the country. In 2007 more than 114,000 Tennesseans were employed in auto or auto-parts production plants. When a Tennessean auto plant produced a car, that car was almost always sent to be sold in another state. And many of these cars were shipped to states where the housing crash was especially severe. So when Floridians massively cut back on auto spending, workers at auto plants in Tennessee suffered the consequences. During the Great Recession, one out of every four Tennesseans working in the auto manufacturing industry lost their job. That's 30,000 Tennesseans who lost their jobs.

It wasn't just auto plants. We see a similar pattern with other goods produced to be shipped to other parts of the country. In 2007 Tennessee ranked eleventh in the country in terms of the share of workers producing goods meant to be shipped to areas outside the state they were working in. From 2007 to 2009, one out every six Tennessee workers producing these goods lost their job. The sharp drop in household spending in California, Florida, Nevada, and New York directly affected Tennessee workers. We cannot be certain of the number of jobs in Tennessee that would have been saved by policy efforts to mitigate the housing crisis elsewhere. But the view that helping troubled home owners in California and Florida was "terrible public policy" from the perspective of Tennesseans is suspect. When it comes to problems associated with levered losses, it does not matter where you live. As we've said, the ripple effects on the labor market mean that we are all in this together.

The previous chapter laid out the levered-losses theory that demonstrates why Senator Corker's argument is flawed. We showed how a shock to spending on Debtor Island would ultimately lead to job losses on Creditor Island through the auto sector. In this chapter, we turn to data to figure out exactly how many jobs were lost because of the destruction in household net worth in the real economy. We also uncover the exact frictions that translated the large demand shock into the biggest jobs crisis since the Great Depression.

Quantifying Jobs Lost

From March 2007 to March 2009, the private sector of the U.S. economy shed 6 million jobs, and the unemployment rate shot up to 9 percent. This was unprecedented in recent U.S. history. How many of these jobs were lost due to the shock to household net worth that we emphasized in the preceding chapters? Our goal here is to use the data to answer this question. As we discussed in chapter 3, household spending from 2006 to 2009 declined by much more in highly levered counties that experienced a sharp drop in net worth. We want to estimate how many jobs were lost *throughout the economy* due to this decline in spending in the hardest-hit areas of the United States.

A natural starting point would be to see how many more jobs were lost in housing-disaster areas relative to areas that avoided the housing downturn. For example, we could show that more jobs were lost in California than in Tennessee. But this would be incomplete for the same reason that Senator Corker's logic was flawed — goods bought in housing-disaster areas were produced all over the country. This presents a serious challenge: How do we estimate the number of jobs lost in areas that avoided the housing collapse because of the decline in spending coming from other parts of the country?

We start by splitting employment in the United States into two major groups: jobs catering to the local economy and jobs catering to the national economy. We call jobs that cater to the local economy *non-tradable* jobs. These are in retail and local services, such as jobs at restaurants and grocery stores. They depend on spending in the local economy. We call jobs catering to the national economy *tradable* jobs. Tradable jobs are those that produce goods that are shipped to other parts of the country. These jobs include building autos or other durable goods like furniture or home appliances. Tradable jobs also include building machines meant for other businesses to use in their production processes. They depend on national spending. This is the same measure we used in the Tennessee example above—Tennessee ranked eleventh in the country on the fraction of all jobs in the tradable sector.[2]

As we explained in the Creditor Island–Debtor Island example in the last chapter, the levered-losses view of employment makes specific predictions about the location of job losses during the Great Recession. We expect to see much larger declines in jobs catering to the *local* economy in areas of the country suffering the net-worth shock. However, we don't expect losses in jobs catering to the *national* economy to be unique to areas with net-worth shocks. Instead, we expect to see the decline in jobs catering to the national economy spread evenly throughout the country. Observing these two joint patterns in the data—non-tradable job losses concentrated in hard-hit areas and tradable job losses spread throughout the country—would support the levered-losses framework.

The auto industry provides an excellent example to illustrate this. The production and selling of autos utilizes *both* tradable and non-tradable jobs. Workers at an auto plant produce cars meant to be sold throughout the country. These tradable jobs are therefore reliant on *national* demand for autos. However, the actual selling of cars needs workers at an auto dealership. At some time during a purchase, a worker must interact with a buyer, even if only briefly. Non-tradable jobs at a local dealership therefore rely heavily on the *local* demand for autos.

The levered-losses framework makes strong predictions on geographic patterns in auto-industry employment during the Great Recession. The data should show many layoffs at dealerships in areas of the country that experienced the largest drop in net worth. We should see fewer job losses at dealerships in areas that avoided the housing downturn. And given the enormous decline in demand for autos coming from hard-hit areas, the data should also reveal that jobs producing autos or auto parts were lost throughout the country. The levered-losses framework predicts layoffs at auto plants regardless of the local shock to net worth.

This is exactly what we find in the data. There was a very strong relation between job losses at auto *dealers* in a county and the size of the local net-worth shock. In counties with the largest shock to net worth, 14 percent of jobs at dealerships were lost. Counties with the smallest shock saw a decline of only 3 percent. We know that indebted households in hard-hit counties sharply pulled back on auto spending. This large decline directly affected jobs at dealerships. In contrast, the decline in spending was more modest in counties that avoided the housing shock, especially at the beginning of the recession. As a result, fewer jobs were lost at dealers in those areas. However, job losses at plants *producing* autos were large *throughout the country.* Job losses among auto production workers ranged from 20 to 30 percent across all counties producing autos, completely independent of local housing markets.

When we put the evidence together, it tells a compelling story. In counties that avoided net-worth decimation, auto sales hardly declined. Jobs at dealerships were safe. Yet workers producing autos at plants in these same counties experienced massive layoffs. These facts demonstrate that job losses in auto production plants were a direct result of the spending shock coming from hard-hit housing areas of the country.

Of course, the exact same test can be performed for all jobs, not just those in the auto industry. And the evidence is pretty clear. The decline in non-tradable jobs catering to local demand was much larger in indebted counties experiencing the biggest drop in house-

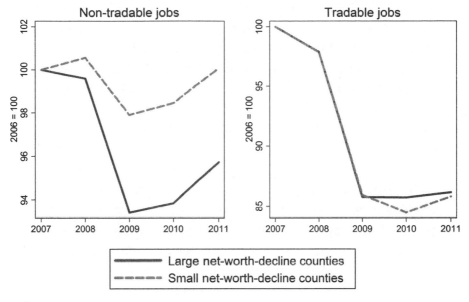

Figure 5.1: Employment Decline during Great Recession

hold net worth. But the decline in tradable jobs catering to national demand was widespread across the country. Figure 5.1 plots the pattern graphically. Just as in chapter 3, high net-worth-decline counties are the 20 percent of counties that experienced the largest drop in housing net worth during the recession, and low net-worth-decline counties are the 20 percent with the smallest drop. As the left panel illustrates, the drop in non-tradable jobs was much larger in counties getting hammered by the housing shock. But the right panel demonstrates how tradable jobs were lost at the same rate across the country. Regardless of whether there was a local housing collapse, jobs producing goods for national demand dropped almost 15 percent across the country.

The pattern in figure 5.1 didn't play itself out in only in Tennessee. Another good example is Iowa. During the housing boom, house prices in Iowa barely rose above the rate of inflation. And Iowans entered the Great Recession with household-debt levels far below the national average. From 2006 to 2009, house prices remained constant in Iowa; there was no dramatic housing bust. Further, total spending by Iowans actually *increased* during the Great Recession by 5 percent. Given the strength of the local economy in Iowa, we shouldn't be surprised that almost no jobs catering to local demand were lost during the Great Recession. Employment in retail outlets and restaurants remained the same. But jobs catering to national demand fell by 10 percent. Despite the strength of the local economy, Iowans working in these industries suffered. This is exactly what we would expect if levered losses in other parts of the country were driving unemployment in Iowa.

The pattern in figure 5.1 underlies our aggregate estimate of the total jobs lost in the U.S. economy as a result of the shock to net worth coming from the housing collapse. Using a few technical assumptions, we estimate that 4 million jobs were lost between March 2007 and March 2009 because of levered losses, which represents 65 percent of all jobs lost in our sample.[3]

Frictions, Frictions

As mentioned in the last chapter, according to the fundamentals view, there shouldn't be such widespread unemployment. Instead, the economy has mechanisms that should make it flexible and maintain full employment, even in the face of a large negative demand shock. For example, in the sectors and locations hardest hit, wages should decline. In the Central Valley in California, the sharp decline in demand should have lowered wages in restaurants, retail outlets, and other jobs catering to local demand. Lower wages should have encouraged retail establishments to keep workers rather than firing them. And as some workers left these industries in search of better wages, this should have lowered wages in the exporting sector of the economy.

In theory, wages would get pushed down to the point that exporting companies would find it profitable to set up plants in the Central Valley. This exporting effect is a standard mechanism emphasized by economists. When a city or country has a collapse in spending, a flexible economy should be able to adjust by lowering wages and making exporting industries more competitive. Another adjustment mechanism should have been migration. Perhaps it was time for workers to pack up and move to other parts of the country with a stronger job market. Economists going back to Joseph Schumpeter have argued that this "creative destruction" process is natural and even healthy. When the economy needs to reallocate its production to new activities, workers move in order to take advantage of new opportunities.

But unfortunately, the U.S. economy during the Great Recession didn't work that way, and unemployment persisted. John Maynard Keynes had it exactly when he wrote: "It may well be that the classical theory represents the way in which we should like our economy to behave. But to assume that it actually does so is to assume our difficulties away."[4] We can't assume that these mechanisms take care of unemployment. We should instead closely investigate why they don't. Put another way, what exactly is it that prevents the economy from adjusting in the way we think it should?

We have already mentioned the zero lower bound on nominal interest rates. But two other frictions jump out from the data: wages don't fall, and people don't move. A trio of economists at the Federal Reserve Bank of San Francisco studied wage growth from 2008 to 2012 and found striking results.[5] Wage growth adjusted for inflation actually *increased* annually by 1.1 percent from 2008 to 2011. And this happened despite the highest rate of unemployment in recent history.

Wages didn't fall because of what's called nominal wage rigidity, or a situation in which wages in nominal dollar terms stay constant. The San Francisco Fed economists examined the change in wages from year to year and found a dramatic spike in the fraction of employees receiving the exact same nominal wage. In other words, employers during the Great Recession didn't cut wages, but just kept them either fixed or increased them slightly. The fraction of workers receiving the exact same nominal wage from one year to the next was higher during the Great Recession than at any other point since 1980.

Looking into the differences across the country in net-wealth shocks, we found some weak evidence of relative downward wage adjustment in the hardest-hit areas. Remember, the hardest-hit areas of the country witnessed a sharp decline in jobs catering to the national economy *and* the local economy. But the relative decline in wages in these areas was quite modest. The declines were nowhere near large enough to stem the rise in unemployment. In the 20 percent of counties that were hardest hit by the decline in household net worth, the unemployment rate shot up from less than 5 percent to 13 percent during the Great Recession. It remained above 10 percent in the summer of 2012, three years after the official end of the recession.

With such dismal economic conditions, workers in these areas had strong incentives to look for jobs elsewhere. But that also didn't happen. In fact, from 2007 to 2009, the population of hard-hit counties grew at exactly the same rate as counties that avoided the housing downturn. For example, in the three hardest-hit counties of the Californian Central Valley, 50,000 workers lost their jobs from 2007 to 2009, and the unemployment rate neared 20 percent. And yet the population actually grew slightly from 2007 to 2009. Despite the disastrous economic circumstances, people did not leave.

Why Unemployment?

The facts lead to one convincing conclusion: The economy was simply unable to adjust to the massive spending shock from levered losses. We've seen that wages didn't fall and people didn't look for jobs elsewhere. But why exactly? A large and ongoing body of research continues to grapple with this question. In fact, it was exactly the issue that motivated Keynes to write his new theory in 1935—in our view, there is still no satisfying answer explaining it.

One explanation offered is skills mismatch. The basic idea is that workers need to be retrained to work in other professions. Charles Plosser, the president of the Federal Reserve Bank of Philadelphia, put it succinctly: "You can't change the carpenter into a nurse easily, and you can't change the mortgage broker into a computer expert in a manufacturing plant very easily."[6] But the skills mismatch story is difficult to reconcile with the widespread employment decline in the economy. Workers in every industry and of every education level witnessed a large increase in unemployment.

Another explanation is that delayed foreclosures and government assistance reduced the incentive of workers to find jobs during the Great Recession. For example, Kyle Herkenhoff and Lee Ohanian argue that the ability to skip mortgage payments without being immediately foreclosed upon acts as a type of unemployment insurance.[7] When a worker loses his job, he can choose to skip mortgage payments, but he must remain in his current home to take advantage of the benefit. As a result, he has no incentive to search for a new job in a different location. Similar arguments have been made concerning unemployment insurance and other government benefits, which in theory reduce the incentives for laid-off workers to take jobs with lower wages. If a laid-off worker receives unemployment-insurance payments, the argument goes, then the wage that will induce him to take a job must be sufficiently high to compensate him for the displeasure of working.

These arguments make sense in theory, but there is surprisingly little empirical evidence supporting them. Jesse Rothstein, for example, examined the effects of unemployment insurance on the unemployment rate.[8] He did find an effect: extending unemployment insurance did in fact increase the unemployment rate during the Great Recession. But the effects were very small, with the extension of unemployment insurance increasing the unemployment rate by only 0.1 to 0.5 percent compared to the overall increase of almost 5 percent. Johannes Schmieder, Till von Wachter, and Stefan Bender studied the effects of extending unemployment insurance in Germany during booms and recessions.[9] They found evidence that the effects of unemployment insurance that discouraged people from finding jobs were actually *smaller* in recessions.

Even if economists can't explain unemployment, that should not cloud the profession's view of the human consequences. They are severe. Steven Davis and Till von Wachter used income data from Social Security records to assess the pecuniary costs of unemployment during recessions.[10] They found that a worker laid off in a recession loses income equal to three times his or her annual pre-layoff earnings over the rest of their lifetime. As they point out, this is a staggering amount. And that is only the monetary loss. The non-pecuniary costs—depression, loss of dignity, divorce—may be harder to quantify, but they are almost certainly even larger.

Persistently high unemployment imposes devastating costs on society. And economists don't have good answers for why it persists. Our view is quite simple: we must work hard to change the economic system so that we avoid the shocks that lead to high unemployment. Once the levered-losses shock materializes, the sharp decline in spending and the painful increase in unemployment are almost inevitable. We must address the problem at the source, rather than expect the economy to adjust when the shock materializes.

Levered Losses: A Summary

We started this book with a robust statistical pattern. The most severe recessions in history were preceded by a sharp rise in household debt and a collapse in asset prices. Both the Great Recession and Great Depression in the United States followed this script. Even looking internationally, we see that the Great Recession was much more severe in countries with elevated household-debt burdens. The relation between elevated household debt, asset-price collapses, and severe contractions is ironclad.

We then presented the levered-losses framework to explain this pattern. The key problem is debt. Debt amplifies the decline in asset prices due to foreclosures and by concentrating losses on the indebted, who are almost always households with the lowest net worth in the economy. This is the fundamental feature of debt: it forces the debtor to bear the brunt of the shock. This is especially dangerous because the spending of indebted households is extremely sensitive to shocks to their net worth—when their net worth is decimated, they sharply pull back on spending. The demand shock overwhelms the economy, and the result is economic catastrophe.

The evidence from the Great Recession in the United States supports this framework. The collapse in the housing market amplified wealth inequality by destroying the net worth of poor indebted home owners. Using geographical variation across the United States, we show that the spending decline was concentrated in exactly the counties where the levered-losses shock was largest. The consequences of the sharp drop in spending spread through the entire economy. Even workers in parts of the country that avoided the housing bust lost their jobs.

But so far we have avoided a central question: How does an economy get into this levered-losses trap in the first place? Or, in other words, what generates such a large and eventually unsustainable increase in debt? We begin our investigation into these questions in the next chapter. As we will argue, debt not only amplifies the crash. But it also fuels the bubble that makes the crash inevitable. If we want to permanently address the levered-losses problem, we must understand why debt is so toxic in both the bust *and the boom*.

PART II
BOIL AND BUBBLE

6: THE CREDIT EXPANSION

For a long time, getting a mortgage on the west side of Detroit was a real challenge. Neighborhoods like Brightmoor, Five Points, and Rosedale Park, among others, have a rich history rooted in the birth of the auto industry in America.[1] Many of the houses there were built in the 1920s, as both blue- and white-collar workers at automobile companies settled in. The area thrived into the 1950s and 1960s, but then a slow decay began. People began moving out, and crime in the 1990s lowered home values. Still, in 2000, these west-side neighborhoods were livable, even desirable places to raise a family. Median household income was $36,000, not too far below the national average of $40,000. Some areas of the west side had very high poverty rates, but others, like Rosedale Park, had poverty rates around the national average. In Rosedale Park, in particular, more than half of the population had at least some college education.

But it was difficult to get a mortgage to buy a home. The recession of 1990 and 1991 hit Detroit hard, where unemployment topped 10 percent. Default rates on mortgages in 1992 reached 12 percent, much higher than the national average of 5 percent. By 2000 Detroit had recovered, but lenders remained wary of extending mortgages: 45 percent of all mortgage applications by west-side residents were denied. Credit scores were dismal. More than 65 percent of households had a credit score below 660, which in most lending markets is considered subprime. Nationwide, only 35 percent of households had a credit score that put them in subprime territory.

In the early 2000s, however, something changed, and all of a sudden it was much easier to get a mortgage in west Detroit. From 2002 to 2005, mortgages for purchasing a home skyrocketed 22 percent per year. The sharp jump contrasted with the paltry 8 percent annual growth in the three preceding years. As one news report put it, residents in these neighborhoods "went from struggling to get loans from banks to having loan officers knock on their doors."[2]

Mark Whitehouse, a reporter for the *Wall Street Journal*, studied the expansion in mortgage lending on the 5100 block of West Outer Drive.[3] Before 2000, home owners relied upon federal mortgage programs or bought their homes outright. But between 2002 and 2006, more than half a billion dollars in mortgage loans from the private sector poured into the zip code containing West Outer Drive. The lending frenzy got out of control. As Derek Brown, the past president of the Detroit Real Estate Brokers Association put it, "Everyone was selling mortgages. There were mortgage offices on every block. One day bagging groceries and the next day selling my mother a mortgage? What the hell is that?"[4]

The dramatic expansion of mortgage availability was not unique to the west side of Detroit. For some reason, lenders were expanding mortgage credit much more freely to borrowers who most likely would not have been able to get a mortgage otherwise. These are referred to as *marginal borrowers*. The expansion of mortgage credit to marginal borrowers kicked off an explosion in household debt in the United States from 2000 to 2007. In these seven years, U.S. household debt *doubled*, rising to $14 trillion. This is how it all began.

Before the mortgage-credit boom, you could pretty accurately predict what percentage of mortgage applications would be denied in a given zip code by looking at the fraction of people in that zip code with a credit score below 660. Zip codes with the highest credit scores had a mortgage-application denial rate of 16 percent, whereas zip codes with the worst credit scores, like the west-side Detroit neighborhoods, had a denial rate of 43 percent.[5] But from 2002 to 2005, credit flooded into low credit-score zip codes. Mortgages originated for home purchase grew 30 percent *per year*, compared to only 11 percent in high credit-score areas. This was the only period from 1991 to 2011 in which mortgage credit expanded so much more dramatically in low credit-score zip codes. Starting in 2007, as default rates began to rise, lending collapsed in these areas, and by 2011 low credit-score zip codes saw fewer mortgages originated than in 1999.

The widespread nature of the mortgage-credit expansion was impressive. For example, low credit-score zip codes in Chicago saw mortgages for home purchase grow by 36 percent per year from 2002 to 2005. High credit-score zip codes saw only 15 percent growth. The corresponding annual growth rates for Minneapolis were 30 percent and 7 percent. For Baltimore, 29 percent and 12 percent. For New York City, 37 percent and 15 percent. Aggressive credit expansion to marginal borrowers was not isolated to Arizona, Nevada, or the west-side neighborhoods of Detroit. The phenomenon was nationwide. During the boom, mortgage-application denial rates in low credit-score zip codes plummeted from 42 percent to less than 30 percent. This is despite the fact that applications for mortgages skyrocketed. This means more marginal borrowers were applying for credit and a higher fraction them were getting approved. For high credit-score borrowers, there was only a very small decline in the denial rate.

How did the flow of credit affect the overall housing market? Before the credit boom, given their inability to get mortgage credit, marginal borrowers were typically renters. Starting in the late 1990s and accelerating during the heart of the credit boom, the U.S. home-ownership rate increased by a full 4 percentage points, reaching 69 percent in 2006. This may not sound like a lot, but it is important to put it into historical context. From the mid-1960s to the mid-1990s, the home-ownership rate remained very steady, between 63 and 65 percent. Compared to this, the rise in the home-ownership rate in just seven years was historic. The increase is equivalent to almost 5 million households owning a home in 2006 that they would not have owned had the ownership rate stayed at its historical average. The increase, however, was as fleeting as the mortgage-credit boom itself: by 2012 the home-ownership rate was back to 65 percent.

Strong Economic Fundamentals?

In October 2005, as the mortgage-credit boom was reaching its frenzied height, then Council of Economic Advisers chairman Ben Bernanke touted recent advancements in the U.S. economy. As he testified to Congress, "On each of the three indicators of the real economy—GDP growth, job creation, and productivity growth— the United States in recent years has the best record of any industrial economy, and by a fairly wide margin." Further, the boom in housing and mortgage markets could be explained in large part by these advancements: "House prices have risen by nearly 25 percent in the past two years. Although speculative activity has increased in some areas, at a national level these price increases largely reflect strong economic fundamentals."[6]

The belief that strong economic fundamentals were behind the mortgage-credit boom is a natural starting point. Why would people voluntarily take on more debt unless they thought they were going to be wealthier in the future? And then there was the aggregate U.S. evidence: mortgage credit was increasing at the same time as workers enjoyed impressive productivity gains. Looking at the aggregate evidence, many assumed that the workers benefiting the most from productivity gains were also the ones borrowing more aggressively. But was this assumption true? Did those who were taking on unprecedented amounts of debt also have improved income prospects? To find out, we need to focus on the *marginal borrower*—or the borrower on the margin who was taking on the extra $7 trillion of debt during the housing boom.

Let's return to west Detroit. From 2002 to 2005, the expansion of mortgage credit to neighborhoods on the west side of Detroit was unprecedented. These areas were filled with marginal borrowers getting mortgages. But when we look at income, a striking pattern emerges: these same zip codes were actually seeing *lower* nominal income growth—average income *fell* by almost 1 percent in these zip codes. If we adjust for inflation, the real buying power of income was declining even more.

This is a startling result. As anyone who has ever obtained a mortgage knows, the income of a potential borrower almost always determines how much a banker is willing to lend. The higher the income, the more debt the borrower is allowed to carry. But in west Detroit, the exact opposite was happening. From 2002 to 2005, borrower income declined, but lenders were willing to give even more credit. When it comes to Detroit, the new borrowers were *not* the ones experiencing high productivity gains. The situation was completely the opposite.

And this happened across the United States. Throughout American cities, credit was pumped into low credit-score zip codes that were experiencing *declining* income growth. Credit was expanding at an unprecedented rate in the United States, but it was not flowing to households with improved income prospects.[7] The direction of the credit flow was particularly dysfunctional during the early years of the mortgage boom. From 2002 to 2004, low credit-score zip codes saw almost flat nominal-income growth, which implies that real-income growth was negative. High credit-score zip codes saw much higher income growth. There was an uptick in income for low credit-score zip codes from 2004 to 2005, but this was after much of the mortgage-credit expansion had occurred.

The behavior of lenders from 2002 to 2005 produced a very unusual statistical pattern: mortgage-credit growth and income growth became *negatively* correlated. That is, areas with lower income growth received more mortgage credit. Our data set spans the years 1991–2011; it turns out that 2002–2005 was the only period in this time frame in which this correlation was negative. In all other periods, mortgage-credit growth was positively related to income growth, just as we would expect if economic fundamentals were driving mortgage growth. But something unusual governed the 2002–2005 credit expansion.

The microeconomic evidence is inconsistent with conclusions that many reached after looking at aggregate data. In the aggregate, mortgage credit grew while the economy strengthened. But the circumstances of marginal borrowers were actually getting worse as mortgage credit flooded into their neighborhoods. The U.S. economy saw productivity gains, but not where debt burdens were growing.

Animal Spirits?

If improvements in income or productivity did not drive the aggressive expansion in mortgage credit, we must look for alternative explanations. One possibility is that the expansion of mortgage credit was a result of "animal spirits" or a bubble in the housing market that had nothing to do with fundamentals. Perhaps, for some inexplicable reason, house prices rose as the bubble formed, and lenders simply reacted to this irrational bubble by extending new credit to marginal borrowers against the rising value of their homes.

The key distinction between a more debt-centric view and the animal spirits view concerns the direction of causality. Was there an initial expansion in the supply of credit that then fueled a housing bubble (the debt view)? Or did the housing bubble start independently and credit merely followed (the animal spirits view)? If the animal spirits view were correct, the expansion and collapse of the bubble would have happened even if there had been no debt at all. In the animal spirits view, debt is a sideshow, not the main culprit.

Can we distinguish between the debt and animal spirits views?[8] Let's start by examining house prices in low credit-score neighbor-

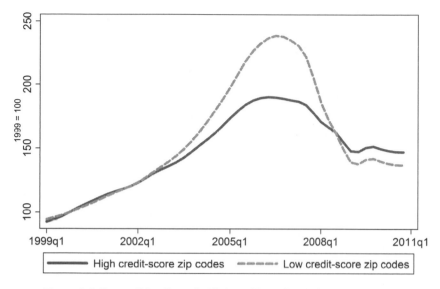

Figure 6.1: House-Price Growth, High and Low Credit-Score Zip Codes

hoods, where we already know mortgage credit was expanding dramatically. At the peak of the housing boom in 2006, house prices in low credit-score zip codes had risen by 80 percent since 2002. In comparison, house prices in high credit-score zip codes had risen by only 40 percent. Figure 6.1 plots this dramatic relative growth in house prices for low credit-score zip codes between 1999 and 2006. (It also illustrates the collapse in house prices after 2006, which was the focus of the first part of the book.)

Did debt cause the bubble from 2002 to 2006, or did it simply follow it? The animal spirits view would point to the pattern in figure 6.1 and say: "Aha! Lenders were reacting to the housing bubble in low credit-score neighborhoods and deciding to lend into them. The fundamental cause of the lending expansion was irrational expectations of higher house-price growth in these neighborhoods." But the debt view would say causation runs the opposite way. It is a classic chicken-and-egg problem, difficult to solve. Is there a way to use the data to tease out which way the causality goes? Yes, there is. But to explain how, we first need a brief geography lesson.

Cause, Effect, and Housing-Supply Elasticity

Empirical economists often face difficult cause-and-effect challenges like the one described above. We attack these problems by focusing on variation in the data that allows us to "shut down" one of the two channels to see which is actually driving the relation. In our context, in order to test whether the growth in debt was driven by the house-price bubble or not, we want to somehow shut down the possibility of a house-price bubble. If mortgage-debt growth occurred despite shutting down the housing-bubble channel, then we can be confident that the bubble did not create the explosion in debt. But how can we eliminate the possibility of housing bubbles? That is where geography comes in.

There is huge variation across America in its land topology. Some cities, like Indianapolis, are built on flat terrain with no major water bodies limiting the expansion of new housing. In areas like these, if house prices rise above construction costs, supply responds quickly by building more houses. We therefore refer to cities with unrestricted, flat terrain as having an *elastic* housing supply. On the other hand, cities with an *inelastic* housing supply are those that lie on hilly terrain or are surrounded by major water bodies that restrict the natural growth of the city. An obvious example is San Francisco. If builders want to construct additional housing units anywhere near San Francisco, they are restricted by both ocean and hills.

The housing-supply elasticity of a city is extremely useful for separating out the direction of causality between the debt expansion and the housing bubble. Elastic cities like Indianapolis are more able to easily build housing units, so house prices can only increase so much. As a result, in these cities, we can effectively shut down the housing-bubble channel. If the mortgage-credit expansion to marginal borrowers occurred even within elastic housing-supply cities—where house prices did not grow, and thus there was no bubble—then we can be sure that the housing bubble did not cause the credit expansion.[9]

We carried out exactly this test in our research, using an index developed by Albert Saiz from satellite-generated data that estimates the amount of developable land in U.S. cities.[10] As theory would predict, housing-supply elasticity had a large impact on house-price appreciation from 2002 to 2006. From 1999 to 2001, inelastic cities experienced slightly higher house-price growth than elastic cities. But the real difference occurred during the height of the boom, from 2001 to 2006. House prices rose by almost 100 percent in inelastic cities in these five years. In elastic cities, they rose only 40 percent. House prices increased in inelastic cities by more than twice those in elastic cities. House-price growth during the boom was highly uneven across the country.

If the housing bubble caused credit expansion, then we would observe a credit expansion to marginal borrowers *only in cities that experienced a housing bubble.* In other words, since there was no substantial house-price bubble in the elastic housing-supply cities, we should *not* observe aggressive expansion in debt in these cities if the pure animal spirits view holds. However, the evidence refutes the predictions of the pure animal spirits view. Even in elastic housing-supply cities with no housing boom, there was an aggressive mortgage-credit expansion to low credit-score borrowers. But there was no significant difference in house-price growth between low and high credit-score zip codes. More credit flowed into subprime zip codes, but house prices did not increase more than average because housing supply expanded.

The presence of aggressive credit expansion to low credit-score zip codes of elastic cities is very important. It proves that the house-price bubble was not driving the growth in mortgage credit. Figure 6.2 illustrates these patterns.[11] The top panel demonstrates that there was no differential house-price growth in high and low credit-score zip codes within elastic housing-supply cities. Despite having the same house-price patterns, the bottom panel illustrates that mortgage credit expanded much more aggressively in low credit-score zip codes. The growth in mortgage credit for home purchases in elastic cities—especially for low credit-score zip codes—had no impact on

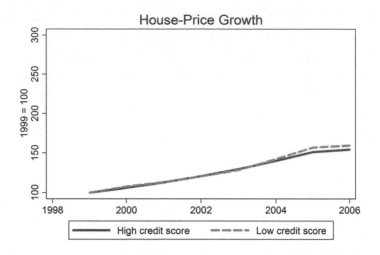

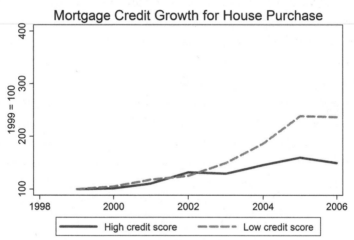

Figure 6.2: Debt and House Prices in Elastic Cities

house prices due to the geography of these areas. However, the situation was different in inelastic housing-supply cities where new housing could not expand with ease. As billions of dollars in new mortgage debt flowed into inelastic housing-supply cities, house prices began to skyrocket. This was especially true for low credit-score zip codes that saw the biggest increase in credit availability.

House prices in high credit-score zip codes in inelastic cities increased by 50 percent between 2002 and 2006. However, house

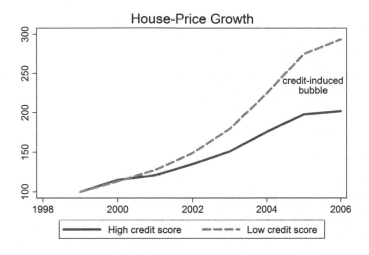

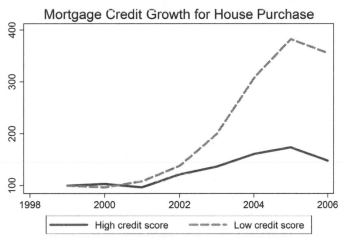

Figure 6.3: Debt and House Prices in Inelastic Cities

prices in low credit-score zip codes increased by twice as much, rising 100 percent over the same period. Aggressive credit expansion to low credit-score areas occurred in both elastic and inelastic cities. But house prices in low credit-score zip codes only increased in inelastic cities due to geographic constraints on home building. Figure 6.3 illustrates these patterns. These facts support the argument that the lending boom fueled house-price growth, not vice versa.

Home Owners Respond

The story we have told so far is incomplete. Before we continue looking into what caused such a massive extension of lending to marginal borrowers, let's recall that households in the United States doubled their debt burden to $14 trillion from 2000 to 2007. As massive as it was, the extension of credit to marginal borrowers alone could not have increased *aggregate* household debt by such a stunning amount. In 1997, 65 percent of U.S. households already owned their homes. Many of these home owners were not marginal borrowers—most of them already had received a mortgage at some point in the past.[12]

Ethel Cochran, an elderly woman living in Detroit, already owned her home when the mortgage-credit boom began. She had bought her home with an $8,000 mortgage in 1982, and stayed in the same home for the next twenty-five years. Between 2001 and 2007, she refinanced her mortgage five times, ultimately having a mortgage in 2007 of $116,000. When the interest rate reset on her mortgage, she was unable to make the payments and faced foreclosure.[13] Ethel's example held for many others. Home owners were not passive bystanders watching house prices rise. Instead, they actively pulled cash out of their homes. So while rising house prices didn't cause the extension of credit to marginal borrowers, but were in fact triggered by it, they did have an effect on existing home owners.

Just how much did home owners borrow when house prices increased? Our research uses the evidence above on housing-supply elasticity to answer this question.[14] Home owners in inelastic housing-supply cities experienced a much larger increase in their home-equity value during 2002 to 2006. The higher house-price growth in inelastic housing-supply cities was not accompanied by faster income growth, population growth, or employment growth. As a result, we can be sure that more aggressive borrowing by home owners in inelastic housing-supply cities was driven by house-price growth, not a change in underlying fundamentals.

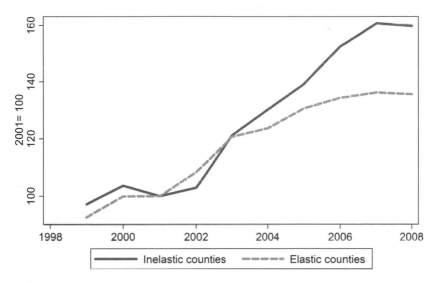

Figure 6.4: Home-Owner Debt, Inelastic and Elastic Housing Supply Counties

If we compare borrowing by home owners in inelastic and elastic cities, we see dramatic differences. From 2002 to 2007, home owners in inelastic counties increased their debt by 55 percent compared to only 25 percent for home owners in elastic counties. Our estimates imply that home owners during the housing boom borrowed on average $0.25 for every $1 of increase in home-equity value. Figure 6.4 illustrates the growth in debt among existing home owners from 1999 to 2008. Borrowing was similar in inelastic and elastic cities through 2003, at which point it diverges sharply. All of the home owners in figure 6.4 already owned their homes as of 1998. So the borrowing represents money being taken out of their existing homes.

The estimates from our research show that over half of the increase in debt for home owners from 2002 to 2006 can be directly attributed to borrowing against the rise in home equity. The household-debt crisis in the United States was created in large part because home owners responded so aggressively when house prices increased. What types of home owners borrowed most aggressively? In our research, we split home owners into the lowest and highest quartiles of the credit-score distribution, and then compared borrowing among high and low credit-score home owners in both inelastic and elastic housing-supply counties.

The results are quite remarkable. For high credit-score home owners, the effect of house prices on borrowing during the 2002–2006 period was small. In contrast, the effect was enormous for low credit-score borrowers. Borrowing for low credit-score home owners in inelastic counties grew by 70 percent from 2002 to 2007; it grew only 20 percent for low credit-score home owners in elastic counties. In response to higher home-equity values, home owners with low credit scores borrowed very aggressively. Our estimates imply that the lowest credit-score home owners borrowed $0.40 cents out of every $1 of increased home-equity value.

Home owners didn't just extract home equity—they spent it. While we cannot directly track spending in the data used in the study, several results suggest that the money was used for consumption and home improvement. For example, many home owners borrowed against their home equity while having substantial debt outstanding on their credit cards. They didn't use the funds to pay down credit card debt, despite very high interest burdens. Further, we find no evidence that home owners drawing down equity used the cash to buy a new home or an investment property. Survey evidence from the Federal Reserve shows that over 50 percent of funds pulled out of home equity are used for either home improvement or consumer expenditures.[15]

Riding the Bubble

The incredibly aggressive borrowing by home owners was instrumental in causing the U.S. household-debt crisis. Had home owners reacted passively to higher house prices instead of withdrawing funds from their home, the consequences for the overall economy would have been far less severe. Most explain the increased borrowing out of home-equity values with the notion of a "housing wealth effect." This argument holds that an increase in house prices represents an increase in wealth for home owners, and home owners respond to an increase in wealth by borrowing to spend more.

But there is a problem with this argument. Home owners should not feel wealthier when the value of their home rises. The reason is that unlike other investment assets—such as stocks—a home owner also "consumes" the home he owns. Everyone must live somewhere, and the price of a home reflects the price of living. Both the value of a home owner's home and the cost of living go up when house prices rise in his neighborhood. The value of his home rising makes him feel richer, but the higher cost of living makes him feel poorer. On net, these two effects cancel out.

To see this point, consider cars instead of homes. Suppose an individual owns a car and the price of all cars goes up 10 percent. Technically, he has higher net worth because the car is an asset he owns. But should he feel richer? Not if he needs a car. While the car he owns has increased in value by 10 percent, he cannot take advantage of the increase in his "car wealth." If he sells his car for the higher price, he will pocket some additional cash. But if he needs a car, then he must buy one at the higher price anyway. As long as he needs a car, a higher price of cars does not increase his wealth. He must "consume" a car, and such consumption is now more expensive. The exact same logic applies to housing.

But we have already seen that home owners did in fact borrow aggressively during the 2002–2006 period.[16] Why? One "rational" explanation that economists have put forward is the idea of *borrowing constraints*. Imagine a young professional couple with high income prospects. They have two young children at home, and as a result the mother has temporarily decided to stay home with the kids. However, she expects to go back to work in a few years and earn a high income. The household in our example temporarily has low income but expects much higher income in the future. This household does not want to cut their spending dramatically just because the mother has stopped working temporarily. The logical solution to this problem would be for the family to borrow. They can use borrowed money to consume more today while the mother is raising the children, and then they can safely pay back the loan when the mother returns to work.

The idea of a *borrowing constraint* is that the couple cannot actually get such a loan. A banker may refuse to grant one. So even though they have good income prospects, they are *constrained* from consuming as much as they would like. How can this constraint on their borrowing be relaxed? One solution is for the couple to pledge something valuable to the bank, like their house. If a constrained couple has access to a house with sufficient collateral value, they can get credit through a home-equity loan. Moreover, if the value of their house goes up for some reason, the couple gets access to more lending. If the couple was constrained to begin with, an increase in house prices allows them to borrow and spend more than before. In this story, the couple is behaving rationally. They consume out of their higher home-equity value because the higher value allows them to overcome the borrowing constraints imposed upon them by lenders.

But here is the big question: Can we explain the $7 trillion of new debt taken on by U.S. households between 2000 and 2007 as relaxation of borrowing constraints? Do we really believe that all this debt was taken out by constrained home owners who expected higher incomes? Does this pass the smell test? In our view, it is difficult to justify the massive increase in borrowing with this story. We already know that the new borrowers during the credit boom of the 2000s had declining incomes, and we've seen no evidence of improving incomes. If a household borrows aggressively today and never sees an increase in income in the future, it is hard to explain their behavior with the borrowing constraints story.

It is much more likely that aggressive borrowing was driven by irrational behavioral tendencies. For example, suppose some consumers have a constant desire to consume immediately at the expense of their longer-term consumption. Such consumers are often referred to as "myopic" or "hyperbolic" in economics.[17] The overspending is irrational in the sense that the individual will regret the decision in the future. In the language of behavioral economics, the individual's future self will come to regret why their present self over-consumed today to leave them a pauper in the future.

Myopic consumers have a tendency to borrow excessively. When tempted with cheap credit or a cash windfall, they will overspend. They may even recognize this personal failing, and they may attempt to restrict themselves through various devices. But the temptation of easily available credit from 2002 to 2006 was likely too much to pass up on.[18]

Whatever the reason, however, consumers who were offered more money by lenders took it. And there were plenty of lenders eager to lend. But why would so many lenders all of a sudden want to lend to the borrowers who were likeliest to default? We have seen that the dramatically increased lending to marginal borrowers was not a result of increased earning power or productivity gains, or even of rising house prices. This is a story that has its roots decades ago and far away from the United States.

7: CONDUIT TO DISASTER

In the early 1990s, lenders in Thailand went berserk. As foreign investors sought high interest rates in what appeared to be a stable and growing economy, a massive inflow of capital from overseas kicked off a lending boom. Total debt as a percentage of GDP in Thailand climbed from 34 to 51 percent from 1990 to 1996.[1] Most of the overseas money went into the Thai financial system, which in turn aggressively lent these borrowed funds in domestic markets. And the lending quickly found its way into real estate. From 1993 to 1996, the volume of real estate loans *tripled*, and there was an enormous construction boom of new housing. Just as in the United States in the 2000s, the flood of lending pushed real estate prices to astronomical levels. Lester Thurow recognized a bubble: "Bangkok, a city whose per capita productivity is about one twelfth of San Francisco, should not have land values that are much higher than those in San Francisco. But it did. . . . Grossly inflated property values had to come down."[2]

Most investors believed that Thai banks and financial institutions were protected by government guarantees against losses.[3] They thought that the government could not afford to let the banks fail — they also knew that many of the financial institutions had strong political and family connections to the government. In 1998 Paul Krugman summed up what happened:

The problem began with financial intermediaries—institutions whose liabilities were perceived as having an implicit government guarantee, but were essentially unregulated and therefore subject to severe moral hazard problems. The excessive risky lending of these institutions created inflation—not of goods but of asset prices. The overpricing of assets was sustained in part by a sort of circular process, in which the proliferation of risky lending drove up the prices of risky assets, making the financial condition of the intermediaries seem sounder than it was. And then the bubble burst.[4]

If we hadn't told you that Krugman was writing in 1998 about Thailand, you might have guessed he was referring to the United States in the early 2000s. But while this story does help show the universality of our thesis, we're not including it just because of its similarity to the U.S. credit boom. In fact, the Thai crisis set in motion a series of events that helped pave the way for the U.S. boom. Thailand is almost 9,000 miles from the west-side neighborhoods of Detroit, but they are bound together in the vicious cycle of debt and destruction.

A Glut of Savings

The collapse of the Thai bubble in 1997 sparked financial crises throughout Asia and the rest of the world, affecting Malaysia, Indonesia, the Philippines, South Korea, and Russia. It even threatened China. When the bubble burst, foreign investors fled emerging markets. They dumped their securities and refused to renew loans.

This was especially dangerous because banks in emerging economies had borrowed in U.S. dollars. Usually, a central bank can provide support for banks in its country as a "lender of last resort." Banks fund themselves with short-term liabilities like deposits and commercial paper. But they invest those funds into longer-term loans. If a bank's short-term liabilities were all demanded at once, it would not be able call back the money it has lent out on a long-term basis. In other words, the mismatch in maturity makes banks vulnerable to a run. Even if a bank is fundamentally solvent, a run can make its failure self-fulfilling.

A central bank can prevent self-fulfilling banking crises by providing liquidity (i.e., cash) to a bank to protect it from bank runs. Just the ability of a central bank to flood banks with cash may be sufficient to prevent runs from happening in the first place, because depositors then have faith that their money is protected.

In the East Asian crisis, however, central banks couldn't flood the banks with cash because it needed to be in U.S. dollars. Without the ability to print dollars, these central banks watched helplessly as the domestic banks and corporate sector went bankrupt as foreign investors fled. Many were forced to seek help from a body that did have the power to provide liquidity in the form of U.S. dollars: the International Monetary Fund.

Of course, help from the IMF comes with strings attached, and forced reliance on the IMF during the crisis left deep scars on East Asian countries. Asians have relatively little representation in the governance structure of the IMF—Japan, China, and Korea all have lower voting shares in IMF decisions than their GDP shares would warrant. Noting this, Franklin Allen and Joo Yun Hong wrote that "despite being one of the most successful economies in the second half of the twentieth century, the South Koreans were forced to raise interest rates and cut government spending. This caused great economic distress." Real GDP declined by 6 percent in 1998, and the unemployment rate rose from 2 to 9 percent. Allen and Hong argued that the high interest-rate policy imposed by the IMF was kept "too long, and it consequently inflicted unnecessary pain on the economy."[5] East Asian central bankers learned an important and costly lesson. To maintain independence and control over their economy, they needed to prevent dollar-denominated borrowing by their local banks. Moreover, in order to fight off potential runs on their currency and banking sectors in the future, they needed to maintain a large stockpile, or a "war chest," of dollars.

Central banks in emerging markets consequently piled into safe

U.S. dollar-denominated assets. From 1990 to 2001, central banks bought around $100 billion annually. From 2002 to 2006, the rate of reserve accumulation just about *septupled*. This led to a breathtaking jump in demand for new safe assets, and foreign central banks heaped money into U.S. Treasuries. As foreign central banks built up their dollar war chests, money poured into the U.S. economy. In theory, this flow did not have to end disastrously. It could have simply pushed down interest rates substantially on U.S. Treasuries, leaving the rest of the economy untouched. But the United States had more in common with East Asia than markets initially thought. The rapid inflow of capital from Asia was not sterile—it turned into something malignant.

Securitization

In *It's a Wonderful Life*, George Bailey, played by Jimmy Stewart, champions the cause of providing home loans as the head of a savings and loan in Bedford Falls. The people he lends to are people he knows, people he grew up with. Released in 1946, *It's a Wonderful Life* reflects a time when bankers specialized in local knowledge about an area and its people. A bank was very much the community's. People put in their deposits, and the deposits were used to make loans. These loans were assets for the banks since, with the repayment of the loan and interest, they provide a stream of income over time.

Savings and loans like George Bailey's served a valuable function, but they were also vulnerable to local or idiosyncratic risk. If a major employer left a bank's community, things could get ugly quickly. Unemployment would make it hard for borrowers to repay their mortgages. The bank would bring in less money, and if things became bad enough, the bank wouldn't be able to lend to others in the community or even return depositors' money. The traditional neighborhood-banking model known to George Bailey was excellent for giving lenders more information about borrowers, but it was especially vulnerable to local risks.

Recognizing this weakness in the mortgage market, in 1970 the U.S. Department of Housing and Urban Development promoted securitization through government-sponsored enterprises (GSEs).[6] Securitization gave local banks a way to sell off their neighborhood mortgages to the GSEs and avoid worrying about exposure to local market risk. In order to minimize the likelihood that banks might sell poor-quality mortgages to GSEs, the GSEs mandated minimum "conforming" requirements like limits on loan sizes and loan-to-value ratios. The GSEs bought mortgages from all across the United States, but how did they pay for them? By pooling all the mortgages and selling financial claims against the pool. These claims are mortgage-backed securities (MBS). With these, interest payments from the borrowers flow through the securitization pool to the MBS holders. The GSEs kept a cut from the interest payments to insure MBS holders against the risk of default.

What was key, however, was that an MBS was not a claim on an individual mortgage—it was a claim on the entire pool of mortgages. As a whole, the entire set of mortgages was extremely diversified, and that minimized idiosyncratic risk. And because GSEs also guaranteed the MBS, investors were willing to pay high prices for GSE-issued MBS. Securitization turned out to be a highly profitable enterprise for GSEs—as long as there were no widespread mortgage defaults.

The supply of GSE-issued MBS was limited to "conforming" mortgages, which met strict requirements in terms of size and credit quality. As the global appetite for safe U.S. debt began to skyrocket in the late 1990s, however, these requirements became a constraint. The increased demand could only be met by the non-GSE private market—if only it could somehow create low-risk MBS from a pool of non-conforming mortgages. The goal was achieved through *tranching*, which slices a pool of mortgages into different layers that define how MBS investors line up to receive payments. The most senior tranche is the safest as it has the first right over payments coming from the underlying mortgages. The junior tranches are paid only if the senior tranche has been paid its promised interest rate in full. So the senior tranche is seemingly protected from default risk by the lower tranches, which are the first not to get paid if borrowers default. The senior tranches of these MBS created outside the GSEs were considered super-safe by investors and certified by rating agencies as such as well. Thus began the "private-label" securitization market.

Securitization was not new, but the explosion of private-label MBS was unique, and it was responsible for satisfying the global demand for highly rated U.S. dollar denominated debt.[7] Private-label securitization was vastly different than the traditional GSE-based securitization, especially when it came to the risks involved. Adam Levitin and Susan Wachter have done excellent work documenting the difference. They note that

> as long as GSE securitization dominated the mortgage market, credit risk was kept in check through underwriting standards, and there was not much of a market for nonprime, nonconforming, conventional loans. Beginning in the 1990s, however, a new, unregulated form of securitization began to displace the standardized GSE securitization. This private label securitization (PLS) was supported by a new class of specialized mortgage lenders and securitization sponsors . . . [the] PLS created a market for nonprime, nonconforming conventional loans.[8]

From 2002 to 2005, private-label securitization soared. As a percentage of all MBS issued, it increased from less than 20 to over 50 percent from 2002 to 2006, before collapsing entirely in 2007. We discussed in the last chapter how 2002–2005 was exactly the period when a massive increase in mortgage credit was flooding low credit-quality zip codes. The timing of the two events hints that they were related. In our research, we directly linked these two patterns by showing that the rate of securitization was much stronger in low credit-quality zip codes compared to high credit-quality zip codes. Securitization transformed global capital inflows into a wild expansion of mortgage credit to marginal borrowers. But it was only possible if the lenders were sure their funds were protected.

Manufacturing Safe Debt

A cynical view of financial innovation sees it merely as bankers fooling investors into buying very risky securities that are passed off as safe. There is substantial research demonstrating that this is exactly what private-label securitization was during the housing boom. Josh Coval, Jakub Jurek, and Erik Stafford show that when investors buying mortgage-backed securities made small mistakes in assessing their vulnerability, securitization enabled banks to amplify the effect of these mistakes. The two most important mistakes made were related: investors underestimated the probability of mortgage default and the correlation of those defaults.[9]

Let's construct a simple example to illustrate what happened. Suppose a bank makes a $100,000 loan to a subprime borrower who will default with 10 percent probability. In case of default, the bank will recover only $50,000 of the initial loan amount by, say, foreclosing and selling the home at a fire-sale price. But the banker must convince the investor that his debt security is super-safe. That is, the investor must be sure the security will never lose value.

Suppose the bank "tranches" the loan into two $50,000 tranches such that the senior tranche gets paid first in case of default. This super-safe senior tranche has zero risk because it will get paid in full even in the case of default. The junior tranche is pretty risky, because there is a 10 percent probability that it will lose its full value: if the borrower defaults, the house is worth $50,000, but that $50,000 gets paid entirely to the senior tranche holder. By tranching the loan into two parts, the bank can finance half the amount it needs from the international demand for super-safe assets.

Can the bank do better? Yes, by combining tranching with pooling. Now suppose the bank makes two $100,000 loans to two different subprime borrowers. The bank combines, or pools, these two loans and then tranches the MBS on the pool into a senior and a junior tranche of equal face value of $100,000. As before, the senior tranche is risk-free. Even if both mortgages default, each house is worth $50,000; as a result, $100,000 of the total MBS will never lose value. Investors demanding super-safe assets will be willing to hold the senior tranche.

What is interesting is what happens with the junior tranche. In the absence of pooling, when there is just one loan, the junior tranche loses 100 percent of its value with 10 percent probability. However, pooling changes the risk characteristics of the junior tranche. The junior tranche is now made up of two underlying loans. If both borrowers of the two loans default at the same time, there is not much value in pooling. However, if the defaults are independent, there is a lot of value. As we will explain, the correlation of defaults among different mortgages is a crucial parameter in estimating how many safe assets can be constructed from the mortgage pool.

Let's suppose the two loans are statistically independent of each other: one loan defaulting has no bearing on the likelihood of the other loan defaulting. In this case, the junior tranche is much less risky. There is only a 1 percent chance (10 percent × 10 percent) that both loans will default and the junior tranche holders lose everything. There is also an 18 percent chance that one of the loans will default, in which case the junior tranche holders lose 50 percent of their investment. But suppose the bank further tranches the junior tranche into a senior "mezzanine" tranche and a subordinate "equity" tranche with the same face value. The mezzanine tranche now has much better risk characteristics than the original junior tranche. While the original junior tranche would have lost money 10 percent of the time, the mezzanine tranche will lose money only 1 percent of the time, when *both* of the underlying loans default. If just one of the loans defaults, the mezzanine tranche won't lose any money, since it has the senior claim within the junior tranche.

As you may have guessed, this tranching and pooling process can continue ad infinitum. As long as the default likelihoods of the underlying loans are assumed to be independent of one another, the bank can reduce the risk of the mezzanine tranche as low as the investors or credit-rating agencies demand. In practice, banks would pool enough loans so that rating agencies would deem the mezzanine tranche "safe," or give it a triple-A rating. So a securitizing bank can create more and more safe assets. In the extreme, the bank can add more loans and do more tranching and pooling to eventually claim that 90 percent of the mortgage-backed securities in the securitization pool are super-safe, despite the fact that the underlying mortgages are quite risky. It could tranche and sell up to 90 percent of its loans to outside investors as super-safe assets, and it would need to put up only 10 percent of the loan value to remain in business.

But the only way this works is if the default probabilities across loans are independent. That is, it works only if one mortgage defaulting is unrelated to the default probability of the rest of the mortgages. So the correlation of defaults is crucial in determining how much of the overall mortgage pool is safe. For example, suppose that all defaults are perfectly correlated instead of independent, meaning that if one mortgage defaults, they all do. If a defaulted mortgage recovers only 50 percent of its underlying face value, and investors know there is some likelihood that all mortgages will default at the same time, they would know there is a likelihood that 50 percent of the money they invested would be lost. In this case, there could never be more than 50 percent of the mortgage pool considered super-safe.

In reality, of course, neither the correlation across loans nor the likelihood of default is known with certainty. People are likely to have varied beliefs about the correlation and default likelihood of the loans. Some investors may be more optimistic than others, thinking either that the correlation is low, the likelihood of default is low, or both. To those who made mistakes assessing these factors, the investments appeared to be extremely safe. Securitization enabled banks to exploit these differences in beliefs among investors and hide the real vulnerabilities of their securities. This allowed them to create and sell more and more genuinely risky securities that were deemed safe, and to fuel the credit supply to low credit-quality borrowers. As Coval and his coauthors put it:

> This ability of structured finance to repackage risks and to create "safe" assets from otherwise risky collateral led to a dramatic expansion in the issuance of structured securities, most of which were viewed by investors to be virtually risk-free and certified as such by the rating agencies. At the core of the recent financial market crisis has been the discovery that these securities are actually far riskier than originally advertised.[10]

Chain of Fools[11]

The problems with private-label securitization of mortgages ran even deeper than exploiting mistakes by investors. If mortgage originators knew that they could unload poor-quality mortgages to investors through securitization at high prices, they could have easily been tempted to ease lending standards and lend deliberately to weak borrowers. In other words, private-label securitization could very well be the *cause* of irresponsible mortgage issuance and fraud. Can we test if this is true?

The answer comes from a couple of very interesting studies by Amit Seru. In the first of these studies—coauthored with Benjamin Keys, Tanmoy Mukherjee, and Vikrant Vig—the authors took advantage of an unusual characteristic of the securitization market. When the market decided which mortgages to accept in a mortgage pool, it followed a cutoff rule. Mortgages for which a borrower had a credit score above 620 were likely to be accepted in MBS pools, while those for which a borrower had a credit score below 620 were much less likely to be accepted. As a result, while a borrower with a credit score of 615 is very similar to a borrower with a credit score of 625, the two differed markedly in the likelihood that their mortgage would be securitized. In economic jargon, there was a discontinuous jump in the probability of a mortgage being securitized at a 620 credit score.[12]

The jump in likelihood of securitization at 620 can be used to test if lenders really took advantage of the ability to sell bad mortgages through securitization. If lenders were just as stringent in reviewing borrowers whose potential mortgages could be securitized (just by having a credit score above 620) as they were for those whose mortgages couldn't (but whose credit score was just below 620), then we would expect all mortgages to borrowers with a credit score around 620 to have roughly the same default rates. If anything, mortgages to borrowers with a credit score slightly above 620 should have a slightly lower default rate than mortgages below 620.

However, the authors found just the opposite. Mortgages originated to borrowers with credit scores just below 620 actually had much *lower* default rates than mortgages originated to borrowers with credit scores just above 620. This means that the mortgages that could be securitized were riskier than the mortgages that couldn't be passed off through securitization. The evidence suggests that securitization directly encouraged irresponsible lending.

How could some mortgages issued to borrowers with roughly the same credit score be riskier than others? Or, in other words, which kinds of mortgages were most sensitive to originator misbehavior in the securitization process? The authors found a particularly strong occurrence of *low-documentation* mortgages, where borrowers did not provide confirmation of their income from a payroll stub or the IRS. When the borrower had very little documentation, securitized mortgages performed especially badly relative to mortgages retained by the originating bank. Banks were much less careful investigating low-documentation borrowers when they knew they would sell the mortgage into a securitization pool. The conclusion is clear: securitization lowered the incentives of banks to screen and monitor borrowers.[13]

The second study by Seru, coauthored with Tomasz Piskorski and James Witkin, demonstrates how private-label securitization blatantly misrepresented the quality of mortgages to investors. They found that one in ten mortgage loans in private-label securitization pools were misclassified as owner-occupied despite being investor-owned. Mortgages made on owner-occupied properties are considerably less risky—a home owner is more likely than an investor to continue paying their mortgage even when the home loses substantial value. Passing off mortgages as owner-occupied when they were not was fraud.[14] The authors show that arrangers of securitization pools systematically underreported mortgages for investor-purchased homes in order to make the pool look less risky. Further, investors in the MBS were systematically fooled—the higher interest rate on the securitization pools where misrepresentation was highest did not compensate them for the risk. The default rates for these misrepresented pools were 60 percent higher compared to otherwise similar mortgages. Investors believed they were buying super-safe assets. Instead, they were buying into fraud. Another striking finding from the study was the *depth* of fraud across the industry. The authors found that just about every single arranger of securitization pools was engaged in this type of fraud. It was endemic to private-label securitization.

These serious problems with securitization fueled an unsustainable increase in mortgage credit. The parties down the securitization chain, especially the ultimate investors, were fooled into taking on risk for which they were not properly informed or compensated. But part of the blame lies also with the rating agencies. Researchers at the Federal Reserve Bank of New York showed that simple, observable measures of risk, like low FICO scores or higher borrower leverage, added significantly to the accuracy of the credit scoring of mortgage-securitization pools in predicting default rates. Or, in other words, obvious information was ignored when credit-rating agencies assigned ratings to private-label MBS.[15]

Inevitable Crash

The expansion of credit to more and more borrowers who were likely to default ended disastrously. Lenders flooded low credit-quality neighborhoods with credit, despite no evidence of better income prospects. Investors buying the MBS fueling this expansion made simple mistakes in their models, and the arrangers of securitization pools exploited these mistakes. Fraudulent practices infected private-label securitization, and credit-rating agencies were either unaware of what was going on or were happy to look the other way. By 2012 lawsuits by investors against arrangers were piling up.[16]

Eager to create and sell profitable securities, lenders extended credit to so many marginal borrowers that they reached a point at which they lent to borrowers so credit-unworthy that they defaulted almost immediately after the loan originated. Once the defaults began to rise, the entire game unraveled, and levered losses kicked in. Research by Yuliya Demyanyk and Otto Van Hemert documents this cycle, showing that the mortgage default crisis "that started in 2007 was characterized by an unusually large fraction of subprime mortgages originated in 2006 and 2007 becoming delinquent or in foreclosure *only months later*" (our emphasis). They also found a "deterioration of loan quality" where "the average combined loan-to-value (LTV) ratio increased, the fraction of low documentation loans increased, and the subprime-prime rate spread decreased." After a comprehensive examination of the mortgage default rates in 2006 and 2007, they conclude that "the rapid rise and subsequent fall of the subprime mortgage market is therefore reminiscent of a classic lending boom-bust scenario."[17]

The rise in default rates during the recession took the country into unprecedented territory. From 1979 to the recent crash, the mortgage default rate for the entire country had never risen above 6.5 percent. By 2009 it spiked above 10 percent. We do not have historical data on delinquencies before 1979, but we know there was no major household default crisis from 1940 to 1979. It is pretty safe to say that in the Great American Recession the household-default rate reached its highest level since the Great Depression. In the same west-side neighborhoods of Detroit that we discussed in the last chapter, mortgage default rates reached almost 30 percent in 2009. More than one in five homes was in foreclosure. House prices fell 50 percent from 2006 to 2009, and they remained just as low in 2012. These neighborhoods were decimated by the mortgage default crisis.

And how did those super-safe mortgage-backed securities at the heart of the credit boom perform? A triple-A MBS originated in 2007 worth $100 in face value was trading at only $50 as of 2012.[18] Investors experienced massive losses on their supposedly super-safe investment.

*   *   *

There is a more fundamental question regarding the blatant fraud and misrepresentation in securitization: Could it still have happened if securitization didn't claim to produce super-safe debt? Would investors have paid more attention if they knew there might be some downside risk to their investments? This is a difficult question. Of course, fraud exists in equity markets as well—Enron in the early 2000s is an example. But the fraud associated with debt-fueled bubbles is almost always more dramatic and more dangerous to the entire economy. History provides example after example of debt-fueled asset bubbles—founded on fraudulent securities—that collapse and take entire economies down. In the next chapter, we dig deeper into the true essence of debt and establish why an overreliance on it is so universally harmful.

8: DEBT AND BUBBLES

Charles P. Kindleberger was a giant in economics. He joined the economics department at MIT in 1948, but not as a freshly minted PhD. Instead, his academic career was preceded by close connections to policy making. He had served as a major in the U.S. Army, worked as an economist in the Federal Reserve System, and was a leading architect of the Marshall Plan in the State Department after World War II. So by the time he arrived at MIT, he had already made a major impact on western European economies.[1] Kindleberger's research style was a bit unusual compared to many of his contemporaries, and this likely reflected his real-world experience outside the ivory tower. Instead of proposing theory, he approached economic phenomena as a natural scientist would. His colleague and Nobel laureate Robert Solow compared Kindleberger to Darwin on the *Beagle*: "collecting, examining, and classifying interesting specimens . . . it was Kindleberger's style as an economic historian to hunt for interesting things to learn, not pursue a systematic agenda."[2] The culmination of Kindleberger's massive data collection on bubbles—*Manias, Panics, and Crashes: A History of Financial Crises*—is one of the most influential books written in economic history. The book is a tour de force: it covers bubbles going back to the tulip mania in the seventeenth-century Netherlands to the commercial real estate boom before Japan's "Lost Decade," to the 1998 financial crisis spurred by the collapse of Long-Term

Capital Management. It represents one of the most systematic and large-scale explorations of bubbles and financial crises ever written.

The Science of Bubbles

Even though Kindleberger didn't set out to prove any one theory, his close examination of the historical data led him to strong conclusions. First, he noticed that the main driver of asset-price bubbles was almost always an expansion in *credit supply*, that is, an increased willingness by creditors to lend to borrowers with no discernible improvement in income growth. What does an expansion in credit supply look like in the context of housing? Imagine a renter walking into a bank and asking for a mortgage to purchase a new home. Normally, the banker will immediately inquire about the renter's income. If the banker deems his income too low to support a large mortgage, she will restrict the size of his mortgage to some fraction of the overall value of the home. In many cases, the restriction will prevent the renter from buying the home he had in mind. Now imagine that for some reason completely unrelated to the renter's income level, the bank decides to give him a much larger mortgage at an even cheaper initial interest rate than what he would normally receive. For the exact same income, the bank is suddenly willing to provide more credit. This will likely affect the renter's demand for housing; he may, for example, choose to buy an even bigger home. If this happens on a wide scale, the increased willingness of lenders to provide credit inflates house prices. For the same level of risk, bankers are willing to supply more credit, and this leads to house-price growth.

Kindleberger noticed this strong pattern in many episodes, so much so that he established the axiom that "asset price bubbles depend on the growth of credit." He gave numerous examples. The tulip bubble in the seventeenth-century Netherlands was sparked by a form of vendor financing, which is debt between buyers and sellers of tulips. The canal mania in eighteenth-century Great Britain was fed by loans from newly established country banks to the entrepreneurs developing the canals. This is what was happening in Detroit. A vast expansion of mortgage credit to borrowers otherwise unable to buy a house fueled an enormous house-price bubble in neighborhoods with many such borrowers. House prices in these areas of Detroit rose by 80 percent in the decade before the housing crash. When it popped, prices collapsed by 60 percent.

What Is a Bubble?

What should be the price of an asset such as a stock or a house? Standard asset pricing theory suggests that it should equal the sum of expected payoffs from the asset. For a stock, this is simply the expected sum of dividends one receives from holding the stock, appropriately discounted for time and risk. For a house, it is the same calculation with implicit rental income, or the income one could earn from renting the house.

Do bubbles exist? There have been many instances of rapid price growth—like the 2002–2006 housing boom or the 1997–2000 Internet boom. These episodes ended in spectacular busts, and it is tempting to call them bubbles after the fact. But what if the price booms were legitimate and based on economic prospects at the time? How can one prove the existence of bubbles without a doubt?

In 1988 future Nobel laureate Vernon Smith and his coauthors, Gerry Suchanek and Arlington Williams, published a seminal paper on the existence of bubbles.[3] The authors conducted an experiment where participants were each given an initial allotment of cash and stocks that they could trade with one another. The experiment had fifteen trading periods. At the end of each trading period, the owner of a stock received a dividend payment that could have one of four values with equal probability—0, 8, 28, and 60—for an expected value of 24 cents. Standard asset pricing theory provides an exact value for the price of a stock in this example. At any point in time, it should equal the expected future dividends from the stock. Therefore, the stock price at the beginning of period 1 should be $24 \times 15 = \$3.60$, and it should decline by 24 cents in every subsequent round. Smith and his coauthors made every one of their participants aware of this calculation to make sure they understood the security they were trading.

The environment in Smith's experiment was a caricature of the true world. It had none of its complexities and uncertainties. There was no uncertainty about when the stock would stop paying dividends, or about the maximum or average payment that one could receive from the stock. There was no political uncertainty, nor any concern about mismanagement of the stock's cash flows. If there were ever a market where the stock price should equal the present value of expected payments, it was Smith's lab experiment. Yet the authors found something remarkable—an outcome that has been repeated many times by various researchers since. Stock prices in Smith's experiment fluctuated wildly, with prices at times deviating two to three times away from their fundamental value. Of the twenty-two experiments conducted, fourteen saw a stock market "characterized by a price bubble measured relative to dividend value."

The results bore an uncanny resemblance to the "excess volatility" phenomena first documented by Robert Shiller in 1981 for the U.S. stock market.[4] In his seminal paper that led to the creation of the field of behavioral finance, Shiller showed that stock prices moved too much to be justified by the subsequent movement in their dividends. This phenomenon was later succinctly summarized by Jeffrey Pontiff in 1997 when he demonstrated that closed-end mutual funds were significantly more volatile than the market value of the underlying securities.[5] Closed-end mutual funds hold stocks and bonds like regular "open-ended" mutual funds. But the key difference is that closed-end mutual funds are traded separately—independent of the underlying securities—and have their own independent price. Theoretically, the price of a closed-end mutual fund should mimic the total value of its underlying securities. But Pontiff found that this was frequently not the case. Prices of closed-end funds deviated from the value of the underlying securities.

All of this suggests that bubbles do exist and that they can make prices deviate substantially from their long-run fundamental value. But our question is more specific: Is there a connection between debt and bubbles? Why are real-world examples of bubbles often accompanied by a run-up in debt, as Kindleberger so comprehensively demonstrated? The idea that the price of an asset should equal the total revenue one expects to receive from it is intuitive and straightforward. Debt plays no role in this calculation. But if the people buying the assets are borrowing money to finance their purchases, as in the episodes that Kindleberger uncovered, is there any reason that the price of a stock or a house should be higher? The price of an asset should depend only on the return one expects from holding the asset, regardless of how the buyer finances the asset purchase. The Kindleberger insight on the importance of debt in bubbles is difficult to reconcile with standard asset pricing theory.

If we want to introduce a role for debt in determining asset prices, we must move away from standard asset pricing theory. We need to consider a world where prices may periodically deviate away from the sum total of their future dividend stream—a world in which bubbles may exist. Perhaps in such a world, debt matters. This brings us back to Vernon Smith. Smith augmented his initial experiment by allowing his lab traders to buy the stock on margin, meaning they could borrow money to purchase stocks. The ability to borrow money should have no impact on the price of an asset under standard asset pricing theory, but Smith and his co-author David Porter found that the availability of debt indeed made bubbles even larger.[6]

Why Does Debt Fuel Bubbles?

Traders buy and sell assets to make money. If buyers know they are buying into a bubble that is about to burst, they won't buy the asset. And if there are no buyers for the asset, then the bubble would not exist. Logic dictates that a bubble can only exist if the buyers are "optimists" (a gentle word for those with "irrational exuberance") or if the buyers believe there will be a "greater fool" to buy the asset in the future when prices are even higher.[7]

We can now start to build a theory of how debt stokes bubbles. John Geanakoplos has investigated how debt enhances the buying capacity of optimists, or those who are convinced that asset prices will continue to rise. By enhancing optimists' buying power in the future, debt increases the probability that a greater fool will indeed be waiting tomorrow.[8]

Imagine a world with 100 identical houses for sale. Two types of people populate this world: optimists and pessimists. Pessimists believe that a house is only worth $100,000. Optimists, on the other hand, believe that the value of a house is 25 percent higher, at $125,000. So optimists are willing to buy a house for any price that is equal to or below this amount. This simple model of the world assumes "differences in beliefs" about asset prices, which, as anyone who has discussed house prices with a friend or family member knows, is a pretty realistic assumption.

So what will the actual price of a house in this world be? It depends on the number of optimists versus pessimists. If there are enough optimists to buy 100 homes, then the sale price of all homes will be $125,000. But if there aren't enough optimists and some houses must be bought by pessimists, then *all* houses must sell for $100,000. The reason for this is that competition implies that all identical houses must sell for the same price. As a result, the market price is equal to the lowest price that clears the market, the price that guarantees there will be at least 100 buyers.

Suppose our world begins with no debt. Optimists have to pay cash to buy a house. Moreover, let's say the total wealth of all optimists combined is limited to $2.5 million. As a result, they can buy no more than 20 houses at $125,000 a piece. The optimists can't buy all the houses, and the price of houses must therefore drop to $100,000 to attract pessimists to buy. Without debt, the price of all houses is $100,000, and optimists buy 25 houses while pessimists buy the remaining 75 houses.

How does the introduction of debt financing affect the price of houses? Suppose we now allow optimists to borrow 80 percent of the value of a house. In other words, for any home purchase, they only need to put 20 percent down in cash before getting the loan. The ability to borrow dramatically expands the buying power of the optimists. For every $1 of cash they put in, they can borrow $4 of debt. They can now leverage their cash of $2.5 million five times to buy houses worth up to $12.5 million. In fact, with the enhanced purchasing power that debt affords, optimists can buy *all* 100 houses in the market. When we introduce debt, the price of a house will be determined by the optimists' willingness to pay. House prices immediately jump to $125,000 each when debt is introduced.[9]

In the world with debt, optimists buy all the houses. They put down 20 percent, or $25,000, for each house, and they borrow the rest. But who is willing to lend to the optimists? Nobody is willing to part with their hard-earned money unless they are sure they will get their money back without loss. Since there are only two types of people in our world, pessimists must be willing to lend in order for optimists to borrow.

Will the pessimists lend? The pessimist thinks that a house is worth no more than $100,000, so he believes the optimist is overpaying. But he is perfectly willing to lend $100,000 to the optimist to buy the house for $125,000. Why? The pessimist has the house as collateral. In the pessimist's judgment, the overly confident optimist will be forced to part with his down payment once the bubble bursts and prices return to their true valuation of $100,000. But the pessimist understands that his money is protected. He made a loan of $100,000, and the house is ultimately worth $100,000.

In this simple example, debt facilitates an increase in the price of assets by enabling optimists to increase their influence on the market price. Ironically, it is the pessimists—even though they disagree with the valuation of optimists—who make it happen. Without help from pessimists, the optimists would not be able to raise the price of a house by 25 percent. This is a crucial lesson when we think of assigning blame after a crash. We are more than willing to blame "irresponsible home owners" who stretched to buy houses. But the house-buying binge was only possible given the aggressive lending behavior by banks.

Debt raises house prices in the example above, but is this necessarily a bubble? We label people in our economy as either optimists or pessimists. Whether the increase in house prices represents a bubble depends on which of the two is right. If the optimist is right, then house prices will remain at the elevated level, and there will be no bursting of any bubble and no crisis. However, if pessimists are right, then the increase in house prices will be temporary and sometime in the future the bubble will burst.

In addition to facilitating bubbles, debt also helps sustain them—for a while at least—due to its impact on expectations. A relaxation in access to debt means that more optimists can enter today *and in the future*. This bolsters the belief that there will be a greater fool who will buy the asset at even higher prices. And the party gets even bigger. The expectation of a bubble growing even more entices speculators to enter the market in addition to optimists. Notice that there is an element of animal spirits in our explanation of the housing boom, even when debt plays an important role. The optimists in our framework can be viewed as irrational buyers of homes, willing to pay more and more because they believe house prices will rise forever. In this sense, the debt view and the animal spirits view are not mutually exclusive.

But the big difference is the role of debt. In the debt view, the bubble cannot get out of control unless irrational optimists are able to get debt financing to sustain it. Further, even *rational* speculators may enter the market if they believe that irrational optimists can still get loans as the bubble expands. Debt plays a crucial role. The distinction is important, because some argue that debt had little to do with the house-price bubble in the United States before the Great Recession.[10]

Why Lend into a Bubble?

As the example above illustrates, lenders are willing to lend only because they are convinced that their money is safe. They are sure that the underlying collateral protects them even when house prices inevitably decline. Debt leads to bubbles in part because it gives lenders a sense of security that they will be unaffected if the bubble bursts.

But what if lenders are wrong? What if they are actually exposed to this risk? The answer is closely related to a phenomenon that Nicola Gennaioli, Andrei Shleifer, and Robert Vishny call "neglected risks."[11] They argue that certain unlikely events can materialize that are completely unexpected, because investors neglect the risks that they could happen. In the context of the housing crash, many investors may have neglected the risk of house prices falling more than 10 percent. During the financial crisis, people investing in money-market funds may have believed that no fund could ever "break the buck," or pay back less than the nominal amount put in the account.

Obviously, such neglect leads investors to make systematic mistakes and exercise poor economic decision-making. But Gennaioli, Shleifer, and Vishny show how the financial sector amplifies this neglect and produces a full-blown financial catastrophe. The key insight is that bankers will create securities that are vulnerable only to these neglected risks. In other words, the securities sold to investors will load heavily on the neglected risk itself. For example, if investors convince themselves that house prices throughout the country cannot fall by 10 percent or more, then bankers will create securities that retain their value in every scenario *except* when house prices throughout the country fall by 10 percent or more. Because these securities look riskless to investors, they will be produced in abundance. This large expansion in the supply of securities that look riskless will fuel an asset-price bubble by allowing optimists to buy even more expensive homes. When house prices do in fact fall more than 10 percent, the result is financially catastrophic.

What is the best kind of security to sell to investors who neglect certain risks? Debt. Debt has the unique feature that it convinces investors they will be paid back in almost every future scenario. An investor buying debt believes what they are holding is safe, independent of the underlying asset they are financing. The financial sector convinces investors that they are holding "super-safe" debt even in the clear presence of an asset bubble. This helps us to understand why Kindleberger found another common historical pattern: asset-price bubbles were often fueled by debt that looked extremely safe. As he put it, "In many cases the expansion of credit resulted from the development of substitutes for what previously had been the traditional monies."[12] Creditors were convinced that new debt instruments were as safe as currency backed by precious metal or government guarantees.

There is another lesson behind the neglected-risks framework: Debt instruments lead investors to focus on a very small part of the potential set of outcomes. As a result, they tend to ignore relevant information; they may even miss blatant fraud. Suppose, for example, investors provide a loan to a business. If the investors are convinced that their loan will be repaid even if the business manager steals some money from the cash drawer, then the investors are willing to ignore the stealing. In contrast, if the investors are equity investors, meaning that they share the profits of the business, they will have a strong incentive to detect theft. Debt convinces investors that they don't have to worry about fraud because their senior claim on the asset protects them.

In a world of neglected risks, financial innovation should be viewed with some degree of skepticism. If investors systematically ignore certain outcomes, financial innovation may just be secret code for bankers trying to fool investors into buying securities that look safe but are actually extremely vulnerable.

* * *

In a cruel twist of irony, Kindleberger passed away in 2003 at the age of ninety-two, just as the mortgage-credit boom was starting.

He did an interview with the *Wall Street Journal* the year before he died. What market concerned him the most? Housing. As the article put it, "The object of his greatest fascination today is the real-estate market. For weeks, Mr. Kindleberger has been cutting out newspaper clippings that hint at a bubble in the housing market, most notably on the West Coast." He wasn't yet certain, but he suspected a housing bubble. He saw one telltale sign: "Banks are ready to mortgage more and more and more and more," he said. "It's dangerous, I think."[13]

PART III

STOPPING THE CYCLE

9: SAVE THE BANKS, SAVE THE ECONOMY?

Spanish housing in the 2000s was the U.S. experience on steroids. During the early part of the decade, house prices soared 150 percent as the household debt-to-income ratio doubled. When house prices collapsed, the home equity of many Spanish home owners was completely wiped out, setting in motion a levered-losses cycle even worse than the one in the United States. The Spanish economy foundered, with unemployment topping 25 percent by 2012. Spanish home owners had even worse problems than their American counterparts. As in the United States, house-price declines destroyed home equity, and many home owners were evicted from their homes. But in Spain a law from 1909 stipulated that most Spanish home owners remain responsible for mortgage payments—even after handing over the keys to the bank. If a Spaniard was evicted from his home because he missed his mortgage payments, he could not discharge his mortgage debt in bankruptcy. He was still liable for the entire principal.[1] Further, accrued penalties and the liabilities followed him the rest of his life. And bankruptcy registers made it difficult for him to lease an apartment or even get a cell phone contract.[2]

As a result of these laws, mortgage-debt burdens continued to squeeze Spanish households even *after* they were forced out of their homes. Suzanne Daley of the *New York Times* reported on the story of Manolo Marban, who in 2010 was delinquent on his mortgage and awaiting eviction. He expected no relief from his $140,000 mortgage even after getting kicked out: "'I will be working for the bank the rest of my life,' Mr. Marban said recently, tears welling in his eyes. 'I will never own anything—not even a car.'"[3] Hard-handed Spanish mortgage laws spurred widespread condemnation and social unrest. Locksmiths and police began refusing to help bankers evict delinquent home owners.[4] In 2013 Spanish firefighters in Catalonia also announced that they would no longer assist in evictions, holding up a sign reading: "Rescatamos personas, no bancos"—we rescue people, not banks.

Even outsiders recognized the harshness of Spanish mortgage laws: the European Union Court of Justice handed down a ruling in 2013 demanding that Spain make it easier for mortgage holders to escape foreclosure by challenging onerous mortgage terms in court.[5] The *Wall Street Journal* Editorial Board—not known as a left-leaning advocate for indebted home owners—urged Spain to reform mortgage laws to "prevent evicted homeowners from being saddled eternally with debt."[6] A number of opposition parties in the Spanish parliament attempted to reform the laws governing mortgage contracts. But in the end, nothing was done. As we write, harsh Spanish mortgage laws remain on the books, and Spain has endured a horribly severe recession, comparable to the Great Depression in the United States.

So why wasn't more done to help Spanish home owners? Lawmakers in Spain made an explicit choice: any mortgage relief for indebted households would hurt Spanish banks, and the banking sector must be shielded as much as possible. For example, if lawmakers made it easier for home owners to discharge their debt by walking away from the home, more Spaniards would choose to stop paying and walk away. This would leave banks with bad homes instead of interest-earning mortgages, which would then lead to larger overall economic costs. The head of the mortgage division at Spain's largest property website put it bluntly: "If the government were to take excessive measures regarding mortgage law, that would affect banks. It would endanger all of the hard work that has been done so far to restore the Spanish banking system to health."[7]

The *New York Times* story by Suzanne Daley reported that "the government of Jose Luis Rodriguez Zapatero has opposed . . . letting mortgage defaulters settle their debts with the bank by turning over the property. . . . Government officials say Spain's system of personal guarantees saved its banks from the turmoil seen in the United States." The article quoted the undersecretary of the Housing Ministry: "It is true that we are living a hangover of a huge real estate binge. And it is true that far too many Spaniards have excessive debt. But we have not seen the [banking] problems of the U.S. because the guarantees [requiring Spaniards to pay their mortgage debt] here are so much better."[8]

Still, the extreme preferential treatment given to banks under Spanish bankruptcy law was not enough to protect the banking sector. Spanish banks steadily weakened as the economy contracted. In July 2012 the Spanish banking system was given a $125 billion bailout package by Eurozone countries. And it was actually backed by Spanish taxpayers.[9]

So did the policy of protecting banks at all costs succeed? Not at all. Five years after the onset of the financial crisis, the recession in Spain is one of the worst in the entire world. If protecting banks at all costs could save the economy, then Spain would have been a major success story.

Saving the Banks

When the banking sector is threatened with significant losses, markets and policy makers are faced with the inevitable question of who should bear the burden. The natural solution is that the banks' stakeholders—its shareholders and creditors—should absorb the losses. After all, they willingly financed the bank and were responsible for managing its investments. However, when it comes to banks, an alternative argument quickly comes to the forefront. Banks are special, we are told by economists, regulators, and policy makers. The government goes to extreme lengths to save the banking system, often at the expense of the common public.

The Spanish story is by no means unique. It was repeated with remarkable regularity in the rest of Europe and in the United States during the Great Recession. In 2008 the comedian Jon Stewart reacted to the bank bailout in the United States by asking a question many Americans already had: "Why not take the $700 billion and give it directly to people—why are we giving it to the banks that created this issue?"[10] So why are banks so special? Why so much urgency to save them at all costs? One possible reason is political: Banks are better organized at protecting their interests. However, before we consider the political explanation, let's review the economic rationale. This requires a basic understanding of the business of banking, which is unique in many ways.

A normal business—making furniture, for example—has a pretty simple balance sheet. The *assets* of a furniture business are the equipment, plants, and machines used to make furniture. A furniture company must buy these assets using money from investors. Some of the money is raised from creditors as debt (through bonds, for example). The rest comes from shareholders and is called equity. Together, the debt and shareholders' equity make up the *liabilities* of the furniture company. A furniture company makes money for its shareholders by producing and selling good furniture and paying off the debt. The money left over represents profits to the shareholders.

If a furniture company performs poorly, the value of its assets declines. The equity holders of the furniture company are the first to lose. If the furniture company does very badly, eventually even the creditors must bear the losses. At that point, the furniture company goes bankrupt. A bankruptcy judge helps decide whether the company should be allowed to continue. If it is, the old shareholders are wiped out, and the impaired creditors usually get an equity stake in the firm that is worth less than the debt claims they had in the pre-bankruptcy firm. So the creditors lose out, but they were aware of the risks they were taking. There is no need for further government intervention or taxpayer bailouts. The bankruptcy process in the United States works very well for non-financial companies.

For a bank, on the other hand, its assets are not equipment or machines, but *loans*. When a bank makes a loan to a home owner, it is listed as an asset on its balance sheet. So the value of a bank's assets is determined by the borrowers' ability to make payments. If the bank's borrowers all default on their loans, the value of the bank's assets plummets. Just like the furniture company, the bank needs money from investors in order to fund its assets—in this case, to make loans.

What makes a bank unique is how it gets funding on the *liability* side of its balance sheet. The primary liability of most banks is deposits. Most depositors don't think of their money as an investment in a bank, but that is exactly what it is. It is a "loan" to a bank that can be withdrawn on demand. The bank does not keep a depositor's money in its vault. It makes loans on the asset side of the balance sheet using depositors' money. These loans will be paid back over years, even though deposits can be demanded back immediately. So the business of banking requires that not all depositors demand their money at the same time, an idea dramatized in *It's a Wonderful Life*. The rest of the bank's liabilities consist of non-deposit debt and shareholders' equity. Because depositors are generally insured and can demand their money back instantaneously, the non-deposit debt of a bank is considered junior to deposits and is usually called *subordinated debt*. Shareholders' equity is the most junior claim and in the parlance of banking is called *capital*.

Suppose a lot of people default on their mortgages and the value of a bank's loans (its assets) drops sharply. The abrupt decline impairs first the shareholders' equity. If the losses are so large that equity is totally wiped out, then subordinated debt takes losses. If the losses are so large as to jeopardize depositors, then the government steps in, guarantees depositors' money, and closes down the bank. Depositors are saved, but equity and subordinated debt are wiped out.

Lender of Last Resort

The primary justification for protecting the banking system is based on the role of deposits in the payment system. Deposits are not just a bank liability; they are the means of settling transactions in the economy. Further, depositors can pull out their money at any time they want. If the value of banking assets falls, spooked depositors may all demand their money when they sense the bank is in trouble—a bank run. Bank runs can lead to even healthy banks going under. For example, even a depositor in a healthy bank will "run" if he believes that other depositors are withdrawing their funds in a panic. The run dynamic is dangerous. It forces banks to sell assets at prices below market value. It can also damage the payment system of a country, which relies on bank deposits: when someone writes a check, it is cleared by shifting deposits from one bank to another. Businesses often pay their workers from deposit accounts. If the value of bank deposits is called into question, the entire payment system of a country may break down.

It is a well-accepted axiom of banking regulation that the central bank must act as a "lender of last resort" to prevent bank runs. It can do so by explicitly insuring bank deposits, as the Federal Deposit Insurance Corporation (FDIC) does, or by lending freely to liquidity-constrained banks. The so-called Bagehot Rule, named after the famous British journalist Walter Bagehot, calls for central banks to lend without limit at a penalty rate, to solvent firms, against good collateral. If a solvent bank faces a run, it can get financing from the central bank to meet the deposit withdrawals. If the bank is insolvent—meaning the value of its assets is even lower than the value of its deposits—then the regulator can step in and take over the bank, which is exactly what the FDIC is charged with doing. Of course, just the presence of a lender of last resort can prevent runs from happening in the first place.

The Federal Reserve took extreme measures in this role during the Great Recession. They slashed the rate at which banks could borrow from the Fed from 5.25 percent to effectively zero. Banks could borrow as much as they liked and for free, as long as they had collateral to post. The Fed also expanded the definition of who could borrow and what classified as acceptable collateral. An entire alphabet soup of new programs was initiated. There was the $150 billion Term Auction Facility (TAF); $50 billion in swap lines for foreign central banks; the $200 billion Term Securities Lending Facility (TSLF); the $20 billion Primary Dealer Credit Facility (PDCF); the $700 billion Commercial Paper Funding Facility (CPFF); and the $1 trillion Term Asset-Backed Securities Loan Facility (TALF).[11] The largest and longest-lasting program introduced by the Fed was the Large-Scale Asset Purchase (LSAP) program. Also known as "quantitative easing," it involves the Fed buying long-term assets that include agency debt, mortgage-backed securities, and long-term treasuries from banks. It has been enormous by any standard. By the middle of 2013, these Fed purchases had increased the size of its balance sheet from around $800 billion in 2007 to a whopping $3.3 trillion.

The financial crisis in the fall of 2008 had an added complication because banks were funding themselves with very short-term financing instruments that weren't deposits. Much of this short-term financing was being provided by money-market funds, which were not explicitly guaranteed by the Federal Reserve or the FDIC. When investors began running from money-market funds in September 2008, the Treasury Department stepped in to guarantee these funds. Their blanket guarantee immediately calmed the market, which shows that the government can and should prevent runs in the financial sector. We view these policies as advisable and fitting within the appropriate role of the government and central bank in preventing crippling bank runs.

Preventing runs requires lending by the Federal Reserve, and in the case of money-market funds during the fall of 2008, it even required lending by the U.S. Treasury. However, this kind of support should not be viewed as a bailout. For solvent banks, the money will be paid back with interest. For insolvent banks, if the government is acting appropriately, long-term creditors and shareholders of the bank will be wiped out. This leads to the primary policy lesson of bank support: *To prevent runs and preserve the payment system, there is absolutely no reason for the government to protect long-term creditors and shareholders of banks.*

Resuming the Flow of Credit

Support for the banks in the United States during the Great Recession went far beyond protecting the payment system. Indeed, government policies took money from taxpayers and gave it directly to the creditors and shareholders. Pietro Veronesi and Luigi Zingales estimated that the equity injections into large financial institutions by the Treasury in the fall of 2008 increased the value of bank debt and equity by $130 billion.[12] Bryan Kelly, Hanno Lustig, and Stijn Van Nieuwerburgh examined options on bank stocks and indices, and found that "a collective government guarantee for the financial sector" helped significantly boost the price of bank equity.[13] So while any policy that would have helped home owners was shelved, governments bailed out bank creditors and shareholders using taxpayer money. Why?

President George W. Bush explained the reasoning explicitly in his September 24, 2008, speech to the nation.[14] It was an impassioned plea to pass the bank bailout legislation, which he assured would "free up banks to resume the flow of credit to American families and businesses, and this will help our economy grow." The banking view goes beyond protecting depositors and the payment system. It argues that bank creditors and shareholders must be protected in order to ensure that banks continue to lend.

If this sounds like a strange argument, it should. The fundamental business of a bank is lending, just as the fundamental purpose of a furniture company is to sell furniture. Few economists believe that the government should promote the sale of bad furniture by stepping in to protect the creditors and shareholders of a poorly performing furniture company. So if banks get in the business of producing bad loans, why should the government step in to protect incompetent bank managers and their creditors and shareholders?

The economic theory behind government protection is that banks perform unique services that are difficult to replicate by any other institution. Ben Bernanke, long before he was chairman of the Federal Reserve, advanced this view most forcefully in his analysis of the Great Depression. In his view, "intermediation between some classes of borrowers and lenders requires non-trivial market-making and information-gathering services." Further, "the disruptions of 1930–1933 reduced the effectiveness of the financial sector as a whole in performing these services." Or, according to Bernanke, bank failures caused lending to collapse, which drove the Great Depression.[15]

Notice the difference between the two independent reasons to support the banking system. In the first, depositors and the payment system must be protected. This does not require any assistance to long-term creditors or shareholders of banks. In fact, it is possible to completely wipe out shareholders and long-term creditors while preserving the integrity of the payment system. The FDIC has done this many times. But in the second, bank creditors and shareholders must be protected because banks have a unique ability to lend.

Did the Bank-Lending Channel Cause the Great Recession?

The bank-lending view holds that the economy would heal if we could just get the banks to lend again. A severe recession is not caused by a massive pullback in household spending; firms and households just need more debt to make it through. This is like trying to cure a hangover with another binge-drinking episode. More debt is not the way to escape a recession caused by excessive debt. Do we really think that households and companies desperately want to borrow when the entire economy is collapsing around them?

To help answer this, there is evidence from surveys by the National Federation of Independent Businesses (NFIB).[16] Proponents of the bank-lending view are particularly concerned about credit to small businesses. Because small businesses rely heavily on banks for credit, they will be disproportionately affected. Large businesses, however, can rely on bonds or commercial paper markets for debt financing. The NFIB is informative because it surveys exactly the small businesses that should be most vulnerable to being cut off from bank lending. The survey asks small businesses to list their most important concern, where "poor sales," "regulation and taxes," and "financing and interest rates" are a few of the options. The fraction citing financing and interest rates as a main concern never rose above 5 percent *throughout the financial crisis*—in fact, the fraction actually went down from 2007 to 2009. It is difficult to reconcile this fact with the view that small businesses were desperate for bank financing. On the other hand, from 2007 to 2009, the fraction of small businesses citing poor sales as their top concern jumped from 10 percent to almost 35 percent. As indebted households cut back sharply on spending, businesses saw a sharp decline in sales. Further, the areas where poor sales were the biggest concern were the exact same areas that saw the worst decline in household net worth.[17]

We also explored how the banking view explains unemployment. As we mentioned in chapter 5, job losses in industries catering to local consumer demand were much larger in counties with the largest drops in household net worth. If a lack of lending was the problem, we would expect these losses to be concentrated in *small businesses*, which depended on bank loans. We found exactly the opposite. Companies laying off workers in these hard-hit counties were the *largest businesses*. This is more consistent with businesses responding to a lack of consumer demand rather than an inability to get a bank loan.[18]

The true image of unemployment during the Great Recession is not of a small mom-and-pop store laying off workers because they cannot get a bank loan. Instead, it is a large retailer like Target laying off workers because indebted households have stopped coming to the store. Kathleen Kahle and Rene Stulz, who conducted the most comprehensive study of the banking view for public corporations, offer more evidence refuting the banking view. They show that, across the board, firms accumulated large stocks of cash on their balance sheets and continued to do so during the Great Recession. If a number of firms were severely constrained in the sense of having excellent investment projects but no banking credit, then we would have expected firms to use their large cash holdings to invest. Instead, Kahle and Stulz found that they did the opposite and conclude that the banking view "cannot explain important features of the financial and investment policies of industrial firms."[19]

The aggregate evidence also refutes the bank-lending view. One measure of stress within the banking system is the spread between the interest rate on short-term financial commercial paper and the interest rate on short-term Treasury bills issued by the U.S. government. The interest rate on short-term financial commercial paper reflects the price a bank pays for obtaining short-term debt financing. The interest rate on short-term Treasury bills reflects the price that the U.S. government pays. When the banking system is under severe threat, the price for commercial paper may be much higher than the price for Treasury bills.

The spread between financial commercial paper and Treasury bills spiked in the fall of 2008. The higher cost of funds for banks would certainly result in higher cost of credit for firms that want to invest. However, the aggressive interventions by the Treasury and the Federal Reserve mentioned above quickly quelled the spike in banks' cost of funds. As early as the end of December 2008, the abnormal spread between financial commercial paper and Treasury bills completely disappeared. The Federal Reserve and the U.S. government successfully stopped the run, which is exactly its primary function for the banking system. There is simply no evidence that the banking system was under severe stress beyond 2008.

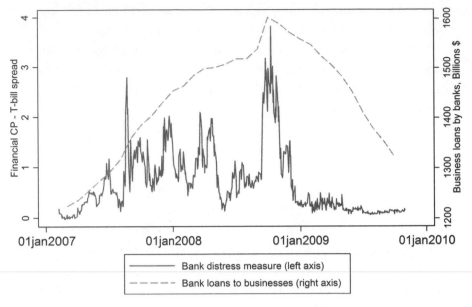

Figure 9.1: Distress and Bank Lending

However, despite low levels of stress in the banking system, bank loans plummeted in 2009 and 2010. This is more consistent with the argument that bank lending collapsed because firms did not want any more credit, which is exactly what we would expect if firms suffered from plummeting sales. Figure 9.1 shows the relation between bank distress and bank lending. If anything, banks actually provided more cash during the height of the financial crisis as firms drew down on their lines of credit. Did we see any sharp increase in bank lending once banks were safe? No. Bank lending collapsed in 2009 and 2010.

Further, as we have shown earlier in the book, employment collapsed in 2009 and retail spending remained very weak even into 2011. Continued weakness in the economy even after banks were saved contradicts the bank-lending view. There is no evidence that banks were under any duress after 2008, but the economy still suffered.

The Power of the Bank-Lending View

Why has the bank-lending view remained so powerful if there's so much evidence contradicting it? The most cynical argument is that creditors wield immense political power, and there is certainly evidence to support this. In research we conducted with Francesco Trebbi, we found that campaign contributions by financial firms led congressional representatives to be more likely to vote for the bank-bailout legislation. This was more than just a correlation. For example, we showed that representatives who were retiring were less sensitive to bank campaign contributions than those looking to get reelected. Some members of Congress desperate to get campaign funds have clearly been bought off by the financial industry.[20]

But we believe there is also a failure of economists to combat this view, which is a main reason we decided to write this book. The bank-lending view enjoys tremendous support among some in the economics profession, and they help lodge it into the public discussion of policies in severe recessions. The entire discourse becomes focused on the banking crisis, and potential solutions to the household-debt crisis are ignored.

Adam Davidson of NPR's *Planet Money* is a brilliant journalist who did some of the best reporting on the financial crisis. In a conversation with Senator Elizabeth Warren in May 2009 (who was then part of the TARP oversight board), Davidson relayed his opinion on the dominant view among economists:

> The essential need for credit intermediation [is] as close to accepted principles among every serious thinker on this topic. The view that the American family, that you hold very powerfully, is fully under assault . . . that is not accepted broad wisdom. *I talk to a lot a lot a lot of left, right, center, neutral economists [and] you are the only person I've talked to in a year of covering this crisis who has a view that we have two equally acute crises: a financial crisis and a household debt crisis that is equally acute in the same kind of way. I literally*

don't know who else I can talk to support that view. I literally don't know anyone other than you who has that view [our emphasis].[21]

Davidson is a top economics journalist who had serious discussions with many economists and knew of no other expert who supported what a brief look at the data would have revealed: that elevated household debt was the driving force behind the dramatic collapse in household spending. This is a failure of the economics profession.

Even in hindsight, the intellectual support of the banking view remains incredibly strong. For example, one of the central arguments we have made is highlighting the difference in the economic consequences of the 2000 tech crash and the 2007 housing crash. As we discussed in chapter 3, the main reason why the housing crash was so much worse is that the marginal propensity to consume out of a housing-wealth shock is much higher—housing wealth is a levered asset held by lower net-worth households. The rich are the primary owners of tech stocks, and they respond much less to a decline in wealth. The larger MPC of indebted home owners is crucial for understanding why the housing crash was so much worse than the tech crash.

In April 2013, Ben Bernanke was asked how macroeconomics should change in response to the Great Recession.[22] To answer the question, Bernanke pointed to this same fact that the housing crash was so much worse than the tech crash. But what lesson did he draw? "Now the reason it was more damaging, of course, as we know now, is that the credit intermediation system, the financial system, the institutions, the markets, were far more vulnerable to declines in house prices and the related effects on mortgages and so on than they were to the decline in stock prices." He went on, "It was essentially the destruction of the ability of the financial system to intermediate that was the reason the recession was so much deeper in the second than the first." Nowhere in his response did he mention that the housing crash was worse because it directly affected low net-worth home owners with very high marginal propensities to consume out of wealth. We have great respect for Chairman Bernanke and his adept handling of the Federal Reserve during one of the most difficult times in our nation's history. But even he continued to believe that an impaired ability of banks to lend was the main reason for the Great Recession. As we have demonstrated in this book, the facts say otherwise.

When a financial crisis erupts, lawmakers and regulators must address problems in the banking system. They must work to prevent runs and preserve liquidity. But policy makers have gone much further, behaving as if the preservation of bank creditor and shareholder value is the only policy goal. The bank-lending view has become so powerful that efforts to help home owners are immediately seen in an unfavorable light. This is unacceptable. The dramatic loss in wealth of indebted home owners is the key driver of severe recessions. Saving the banks won't save the economy. Instead, bolstering the economy by attacking the levered-losses problem directly would save the banks.

We don't believe the banks are unimportant. In fact, research we conducted before the Great Recession found that banks play a crucial role in intermediating credit. Some of the decline in the economy during the heart of the financial crisis was a result of problems in the banking sector. But the bank-lending view has become so powerful that it has killed many efforts that could have helped mitigate the crushing household-debt burdens that drove the Great Recession. Policy makers have consistently viewed assistance to indebted households as a zero-sum game: helping home owners means hurting banks, and hurting banks would be the worst thing for the economy.

Housing policy during the Obama administration was severely hampered by strong adherence to the banking view. Clea Benson at Bloomberg covered President Obama's approach to housing and came to the conclusion that "while his [housing] plan was undermined in part by the weak U.S. economic recovery, it also lacked broad and aggressive measures. Relief programs have tinkered around the edges of the housing finance system *because Obama's advisers chose early on not to expend political capital forcing banks to forgive mortgage debt*" (our emphasis).[23]

The same narrative emerges from Kristin Roberts and Stacy Kaper's extensive review of housing policy during the Great Recession that appeared in the *National Journal*. From the very beginning of the Obama administration, they wrote, a guiding principle in housing policy was that "the government would not force banks to modify loans, and any changes made to mortgage terms would have to work for investors as well as homeowners." Members of the administration "were motivated time and again by a heartfelt need to support banks still struggling to emerge from the financial crisis, and to contain the losses faced by lenders and bond investors."[24]

In the levered-losses view, using taxpayer money to bail out bank creditors and shareholders while ignoring the household-debt problem is counterproductive. Remember, the decline in consumer spending is driven by low net-worth indebted home owners. Bank creditors and shareholders are the richest households in the economy. A bailout of bank creditors and shareholders provides valuable taxpayer funds to a group with a very low marginal propensity to consume. The bank-lending view advocates taxpayer gifts to exactly the households that need relief the least.

The real reason banks are suffering is that the recession was caused by a collapse in household spending. If we want to save the banks, the better approach would be to attack the household-leverage problem directly.

10: FORGIVENESS

Rick Santelli left no doubt on his stance toward helping indebted home owners. The CNBC reporter delivered a rant on the floor of the Chicago Board of Trade in February 2009, just as the new Obama administration was settling in. "How about this, Mr. President and new administration?" he asked. "Why don't you put up a website to have people vote on the Internet as a referendum to see if we really want to subsidize the losers' mortgages?" He turned to the traders on the floor, asking, "How many people want to pay for your neighbor's mortgage that has an extra bathroom and can't pay their bills? Raise their hand." The traders loudly booed. One of the traders responded, "It's a moral hazard!" The Santelli rant struck a nerve; it is suspected to have played an important role in founding the Tea Party movement that dominated the 2010 midterm elections. Americans were outraged that their irresponsible neighbors were being bailed out.[1]

The sad fact is that when Santelli made his speech, very few home owners had received debt relief. And they didn't get a bailout afterward, either. Despite the biggest housing collapse in post–Great Depression American history, indebted home owners were left drowning underwater with only minimal assistance from the government.

An attempt at helping indebted home owners first came in the summer of 2008, when Congress passed the American Housing

Rescue and Foreclosure Prevention Act. It provided the Federal Housing Administration with $300 billion to encourage the private sector to reduce principal balances on mortgages. It was supposed to help 400,000 home owners avoid foreclosure. By December 2008, it attracted only 312 applications. None of the money was spent. The Secretary of Housing and Urban Development Steve Preston put the blame squarely on Congress for a poorly constructed bill and called the legislation a failure.[2]

During negotiations on the Emergency Economic Stabilization Act in September 2008, many legislators demanded that TARP funds be used to help home owners as well as banks. The legislation set up a number of programs to ease household-debt burdens, including the Home Affordable Modification Program. It was supposed to help 3 to 4 million at-risk home owners avoid foreclosure by easing mortgage terms. Five years later, it had led to only 860,000 permanent modifications.[3]

The actual funds spent reducing household-debt burdens from TARP were tiny compared to the bank bailouts. The Special Inspector General's first quarter 2013 report on TARP showed that the Treasury spent less than 2 percent of TARP funds on home-owner relief programs. In contrast, it spent 75 percent of TARP funds to rescue financial institutions. As the SIGTARP report pointed out, one single bank—the PNC Financial Services Group—received as much support as *all* home owners in the entire country. The SIGTARP report noted the disparity between the treatment of banks and indebted home owners: "Treasury pulled out all the stops for the largest financial institutions, and it must do the same for homeowners."[4]

Even members of the Obama administration have expressed frustration that they didn't do more on housing and household debt. Lawrence Summers, who was President Obama's powerful top economic adviser, admitted in 2012 that "if we made a serious mistake, the best arguments would be around questions about housing." Former budget director Peter Orszag said that failure to address housing problems was "a major policy error." In 2012 Christina Romer, the former chair of the Council of Economic Advisers, said that more efforts were needed to help reduce principal balances for underwater home owners.[5] The *National Journal*'s review of the Obama administration's housing policy by Kristin Roberts and Stacy Kaper pulled no punches. They summarized the housing response as "tepid, half-hearted, and conflicted policies. . . . It was a disastrous approach that did little for a market in free fall or for the millions of Americans still underwater and facing foreclosure." Further, "although the federal government would spend reams of cash to stanch, to some degree, losses suffered by the financial sector, the auto industry, and state and local governments, suffering homeowners would see no relief. . . . Their bailout never arrived."[6]

Economic Rationale for Intervention

To justify government intervention, economists rely on the notion of *market failures*. There were very clear market failures that warranted the facilitation of mortgage-debt restructuring during the Great Recession. They can be split into *microeconomic* and *macroeconomic* categories. Let's start with the microeconomic ones.

Foreclosures are bad for everyone. They kick families out of their homes, depress house prices, and elicit major losses for lenders, who typically want to avoid foreclosure except in extreme circumstances. When house prices crash, home owners and lenders have a strong incentive to return to the bargaining table and modify the loans. Unfortunately, the securitization of mortgages during the housing boom made it very difficult to renegotiate mortgages, even when everyone would have been better off by doing so. Remember, mortgages during the boom were pooled and tranched into mortgage-backed securities (as described in chapter 7). A servicer represented the holders of MBS, and they were responsible for administering and renegotiating mortgages. When house prices crashed, home owners could not turn to a bank to renegotiate the mortgage—no bank held the mortgage. Instead, they were forced to deal with a servicer, who was often unresponsive.

But securitization impeded efficient renegotiation of mortgages for other reasons, as well.[7] Most directly, some securitization contracts explicitly prohibited servicers from renegotiating. Others imposed severe limits on servicers. Research suggests that up to 40 percent of private-label MBS contained some restriction limiting the servicer's ability to modify mortgages in the securitization pool.[8] Even when it wasn't explicitly prohibited, the structure within securitization pools made it difficult to get all parties to agree to writing down principal, even if most would benefit. The Trust Indenture Act of 1939 stipulated that "modifying the economic terms of RMBS required the consent of 100 percent of their holders."[9] If even one MBS holder decided it would be better to foreclose than to renegotiate, the servicer's hands would be tied. More generally, the securitization contracts put the servicers in a very difficult position. As John Geanakoplos put it: "Modifying the loans has different effects on different bondholders. It has proved difficult to modify loans in a way that pleases everyone . . . there is a complex negotiation that is not taking place, and the government needs to intervene to break an impasse for the public good."[10]

Further, securitization arrangements did not properly incentivize servicers to do the hard work of modification, even when it was to the benefit of the MBS holders. For example, most agreements compensated the servicer for costs of foreclosure, but not for expenses associated with modification.[11] Given the magnitude of the mortgage default crisis, servicers needed to set up reasonably large operations to renegotiate mortgages. But their compensation arrangements did not give them reasons to do so. A research study of the Home Affordable Modification Program (one of the attempts to help indebted home owners mentioned above) by a group of top academic and regulatory economists showed these problems clearly. The HAMP was supposed to give strong incentives to servicers to modify mortgage terms. However, the authors argued that the main impediment to successful implementation was the inability of servicers to handle large volumes. They conclude by saying that servicers' "low renegotiation activity—which is also observed before the program—reflects servicer-specific factors that appear to be related to their preexisting organizational capabilities."[12]

And there is more serious research that strongly supports the argument that securitization impeded efficient renegotiation. Tomasz Piskorski, Amit Seru, and Vikrant Vig found that delinquent mortgages were more likely to end up in foreclosure if they were held in a securitization pool rather than on the balance sheet of an individual bank.[13] The research design of their study ensured that the mortgages considered were identical in every other aspect except for whether the mortgage was in a securitization pool or not. Sumit Agarwal, Gene Amromin, Itzhak Ben-David, Souphala Chomsisengphet, and Douglas Evanoff used a separate data set but reached a similar conclusion: securitization impeded the ability of home owners to renegotiate their mortgages. Further, they showed that bank-held loans that were renegotiated had much better performance than mortgages in a securitization pool. Not only were mortgages more likely to be renegotiated if they were not in a securitization pool, but they were also less likely to see re-default and were therefore more profitable to the lender.[14]

Securitization was not the only reason we saw too little mortgage renegotiation. Another is that servicers wanted to solidify a reputation as a "tough guy" to prevent more widespread defaults. Even if it made economic sense for a servicer to reduce principal on a given mortgage, the servicer chose not to out of fear that other borrowers would strategically stop paying in order to get a debt write-down as well.[15] These strategic default problems put a lid on private renegotiations even when more restructuring would have improved the economy. Because it discouraged the efficient renegotiation of mortgages, the mortgage market structure in 2007 was horribly suited for the collapse in house prices in the Great Recession.

Macroeconomic Failures

Perhaps no other government official did more harm to mortgage-debt write-down efforts than Edward DeMarco, the acting director of the Federal Housing Finance Agency, which oversees the government-sponsored enterprises (GSEs) of Freddie Mac and Fannie Mae. Despite evidence from his own researchers that principal reduction would have large benefits to both the GSEs and taxpayers, DeMarco obstinately refused to budge on the issue.[16] His strong stance against principal reduction earned the ire of Secretary of the Treasury Timothy Geithner, who wrote a public letter to DeMarco in July 2012 condemning his stalling on principal-reduction efforts.[17] In 2013 a prominent group of state attorney generals took the unusual step of publicly calling on President Obama to fire DeMarco because of his refusal to help reduce mortgage-debt burdens for underwater home owners.[18] This was not a partisan issue. Even Glenn Hubbard, top economic adviser to 2012 Republican presidential nominee Mitt Romney, assailed the incompetence of the FHFA in implementing principal write-down and refinancing efforts.[19]

DeMarco justified his stance against principal reduction with a very narrow focus on the bottom line of the GSEs. Even within this narrow dimension, his own researchers contradicted him. But there was an even bigger flaw: his narrow view ignored the *macroeconomic failures* that a government official in his position should have recognized. Even if aggressive principal reduction had hurt the bottom line of the GSEs, it may still have been in the *national interest* to alleviate household-debt burdens. Recall from chapter 3 that the marginal propensity to consume out of wealth during the Great Recession was the highest for low-income, highly levered households. As we discussed in that chapter, the fall in household spending from 2006 to 2009 was severe in part because wealth losses were concentrated on exactly these households.

Principal forgiveness would have resulted in a more equal sharing of the losses associated with the housing crash. Debtors *and* creditors would have more evenly absorbed the shock to wealth, instead of debtors bearing almost all the pain. Given that creditors tend to have high income and low leverage whereas borrowers tend to have low income and high leverage, a more equal sharing of losses would have transferred wealth from people with very low marginal propensities to consume to people with very high marginal propensities to consume. This would have boosted overall demand. A creditor barely cuts spending when a dollar is taken away, but a borrower spends aggressively out of a dollar gained. As we highlighted in chapter 3, indebted households had MPCs out of wealth that were three to five times larger than others'.

Economic policy should not always try to get dollars to households with the highest MPC. But severe recessions are special circumstances because macroeconomic failures prevent the economy from reacting to a severe drop in demand. We outlined some of these macroeconomic market failures in chapter 4, which include the zero lower bound and other rigidities. When such failures prevent the economy from adjusting to such a large decline in consumption, government policy should do what it can to boost household spending. Debt forgiveness is exactly one such policy, and arguably the most effective, given its role in reducing foreclosures and the very large differences in MPCs between creditors and debtors.[20]

One might argue that it is not the job of a private bank to voluntarily write down mortgage principal for the wider good of the public. However, DeMarco's position as head of the GSEs was different. The GSEs by this time were a public entity and effectively belonged to taxpayers. It was DeMarco's responsibility to act in the wider interest of the American public and pursue principal writedowns. Unfortunately, that wasn't the case, and the failure to respond adequately to the housing crisis was likely the biggest policy mistake of the Great Recession.

Some have argued that debt restructuring would have had little benefit because spending out of housing wealth, even for indebted households, is too small to have made a significant contribution to GDP.[21] This is a narrow view. As we explained in the first part of the book, the collapse in spending by indebted households infected the *entire* economy through foreclosures and employment. The evidence from the county-level analysis we discussed in those chapters demonstrates the centrality of elevated household-debt levels in explaining the severity of the recession. An aggressive restructuring of household debt early in the Great Recession would have slowed plummeting house prices and supported jobs. The benefits would have been far larger than just the additional spending by indebted households. In the final chapter of the book, we consider a scenario in which housing losses from 2006 to 2009 had been automatically more evenly distributed between creditors and home owners, and we show quantitatively that the Great Recession would have been only a mild recession under such a scenario.

As mentioned in the previous chapter, the overwhelming bias of economists and policy makers during the heart of the Great Recession was toward saving banks at all costs. But as the economic slump continued, the benefits of more aggressive household-debt write-downs found their way into the economic mainstream. In 2011 Harvard economist and president emeritus of the National Bureau of Economic Research Martin Feldstein wrote that the "only real solution" to the housing mess was "permanently reducing the mortgage debt hanging over America."[22] Top economists who met with the president and vice president in 2011 said that the president "could have significantly accelerated the slow economic recovery if he had better addressed the overhang of mortgage debt left when housing prices collapsed."[23] In 2011 Carmen Reinhart concluded that "a restructuring of U.S. household debt, including debt forgiveness for low-income Americans, would be most effective in speeding economic growth."[24]

Lessons from History

There are sound microeconomic and macroeconomic reasons for government intervention to restructure household debt during a levered-losses episode. U.S. policy makers in the past acted to soften the blow on debtors. In fact, the policy response on household debt during the Great Recession was an outlier.

The first economic crisis to hit the United States was in the late 1810s, and it shares many similarities with our latest experience. Two main forces during the early part of that decade fueled urban and rural real estate prices. The first was high commodity prices, which were driven by strong European demand after a series of poor harvests overseas. The second was an unsustainable expansion of credit by new banks issuing their own currency notes. The situation was ripe for levered-losses crash. As the historian Murray N. Rothbard put it: "The rise in export values and the monetary and credit expansion led to a boom in urban and rural real estate prices, speculation in the purchase of public lands, and rapidly growing indebtedness by farmers for projected improvements."[25]

The tipping point came in 1819, when the Bank of the United States precipitated a deflationary crisis by calling in funds from banks to pay off government debt coming due. Simultaneously, commodity prices collapsed due to weaker demand from Europe. The price of cotton fell 50 percent from January 1818 to June 1819.[26] These two forces led to a collapse in real estate prices, and leverage exacerbated the problems. As Rothbard notes, "One of the most striking problems generated by the panic [of 1819] was the plight of debtors. Having borrowed heavily during the preceding boom, they were confronted now with calls for repayment and falling prices, increasing the burden of their debts."[27] Rothbard wrote these words in 1962, but he easily could have been describing the Great Recession.

That is where the similarities end. In contrast to the Great Recession, governments in 1819 at the state and national level responded aggressively to the needs of indebted individuals, in particular farmers. Many state governments immediately imposed moratoria on debt payments and foreclosures.[28] At the national level, an important group of debtors were farmers who had purchased public land using debt from the federal government.[29] In 1818–1820, Congress passed postponement laws allowing debtors to delay making payments. In 1820 William H. Crawford, the secretary of treasury under President James Monroe, proposed legislation that would (1) allow farmers to relinquish only some of their land while retaining title in the rest, (2) forgive 25 to 37.5 percent of the total debt, and (3) give permission to borrowers to pay sums due in ten equal annual installments without interest.[30] During the debate on the legislation, Senator Ninian Edwards of Illinois passionately defended debtors. As Rothbard writes, "Edwards went into great detail to excuse the actions of the debtors. The debtors, like the rest of the country, had been infatuated by the short-lived 'artificial and fictitious prosperity.' They thought that the prosperity would be permanent. . . . He also pointed to the distress prevailing among the debtors . . . all highlighting the need for governmental relief."[31] The legislation easily passed Congress.

The Great Depression ultimately witnessed strong government efforts to assist debtors. The most famous of these programs was the Home Owners' Loan Corporation. The HOLC was a taxpayer-funded government bank that actually bought mortgage loans from private lenders and then made the terms more favorable to borrowers. The benefits to home owners were substantial. Without a modified loan, most home owners could not have made principal repayments and would have ended up in foreclosure. Further, the modified loans sometimes reduced principal and almost always reduced the interest rate and extended the maturity. While most mortgages originated before the Great Depression had a maturity of only five years, HOLC mortgages had a maturity of fifteen years.[32] The scale of the HOLC was enormous. By 1936, 10 percent of American home owners were borrowers from the HOLC. The most extensive research of the HOLC to date is a recent book by Price Fishback, Kenneth Snowden, and Jonathan Rose, *Well Worth Saving*. They conclude by pointing out that while the HOLC involved some losses to taxpayers, the benefits to both lenders and home owners were significantly larger.[33]

Another dramatic Depression-era government intervention had

to do with gold. Almost all long-term debt contracts in the United States at the time included a clause giving creditors the right to demand payment in gold. When the United States went off the gold standard in 1933, the dollar was worth far less in gold than it had been. As a result, creditors all wanted to be paid the original amount back in gold. But the gold clause in debt contracts was abrogated by Congress. This meant borrowers could pay back in dollars that were worth far less in real terms than what they had borrowed. As former Federal Reserve governor Randall Kroszner points out, "The abrogation of these clauses was tantamount to a debt jubilee." When Congress did this, it was equivalent to a one-time massive debt-forgiveness program on the order of the entire GDP of the country.[34]

Interestingly, the effects of the gold-clause abrogation were quite positive for both borrowers *and* lenders. As Kroszner demonstrates, both equity prices and bond prices *rose* when the Supreme Court upheld the congressional action. In other words, *debt forgiveness actually made creditors better off*. It is likely that we would have reached a similar outcome during the Great Recession had the government more aggressively facilitated the restructuring of household debt.

The Specifics

An often-made argument is that the Great Recession was inherently different from past episodes, and these differences made debt forgiveness more complicated from both political and implementation standpoints. There is truth in this statement, which is why we propose policies in chapter 12 to avoid getting into such a big mess in the first place. But it is important to highlight that there were many debt write-down proposals that could have been implemented and would have significantly accelerated the recovery.

In October 2008, John Geanakoplos and Susan Koniak pointed out inherent flaws in securitization that made efficient renegotiation of mortgages difficult.[35] They proposed taking mortgage servicers out of the picture and instead giving government-appointed trustees the right to renegotiate mortgages that had been sold into securitization, regardless of what the contracts with MBS investors said. The modifications would take place between home owners and trustees, and would be allowed to take place only if they made economic sense. As they wrote, "The blind trustees would consider, loan by loan, whether a reworking would bring in more money than a foreclosure." While such government intervention would have violated the contracts signed between servicers and MBS investors, these contracts were not designed to deal with such a massive rise in mortgage delinquencies and therefore needed to be scrapped anyway. Further, such an intervention would have cost very little taxpayer money—only the trustees would have needed to be compensated. The proposal would have allowed for more efficient renegotiation of mortgages that would have reduced debt and left both home owners and MBS investors better off—at little taxpayer cost.

Another proposal put forth at the beginning of the housing crisis was the allowance of mortgage cram-downs by judges in Chapter 13 bankruptcy. In a Chapter 13 bankruptcy, an individual with too much debt submits a debt payback plan to a bankruptcy trustee in order to reduce his overall debt burden.[36] Chapter 13 bankruptcy allows people to reduce debt that is not explicitly secured by some collateral. Credit card debt falls into this category. However, in the case of a mortgage on a principal residence, Chapter 13 does not allow for a reduction of the principal balance and does not prevent foreclosures.[37]

The week before the 2008 election, soon-to-be Vice President Joseph Biden told Floridians, "If we can help Wall Street, folks, we sure can help Silver Springs Boulevard right here in Ocala. That's why we believe we should reform our bankruptcy laws, giving bankruptcy judges the authority to reduce the amount of principal owed, give them the authority to go out and reset the terms of the mortgage so people can stay in their homes."[38] Barack Obama had sponsored mortgage cram-down legislation as a U.S. senator and endorsed it as a presidential candidate in a speech in Arizona.[39] But a 2012 *New York Times* article by Binyamin Appelbaum noted that the president "repeatedly pressed the pause button" when it came to enacting legislation.[40] A watered-down version failed to pass the Senate in early 2009.

Two widely respected housing experts were in strong support of mortgage cram-downs — Doris Dungy and Bill McBride of the *Calculated Risk* website. The blog is one of the most read in economics and was among the first to recognize the dangers of the debt-fueled housing bubble. As early as October 2007, Dungy made a strong case to immediately allow judges to write down mortgage debt in bankruptcy.[41] The benefits of cram-down, according to Dungy, were "not just as a relief measure for debtors but as a disincentive for lenders relaxing credit standards too far."[42] In August 2012, McBride noted that "cram-downs in bankruptcy are still an appropriate policy."[43]

Mortgage cram-downs would have had major benefits for the economy.[44] Most research indicates that principal write-down is the most effective way of curing default permanently.[45] Principal write-downs give owners an equity stake in the home and significantly lower payments, both of which provide strong incentives to remain solvent. Banks that held mortgages on their own balance sheet were most likely to write down principal, and these modified mortgages also saw the lowest re-default rates.[46]

In hindsight, current and former Obama administration officials have conceded that failing to write down mortgage debt more aggressively was a mistake. As the *National Journal* points out, "Two of the sidelined options — a policy known as cramdown and a broad-based reduction of principal owed on loans — could have been game-changers, according to economists inside and outside the administration. Even high-level policy officials and advisers readily concede that those options were missed opportunities."[47] The article quotes Secretary of Housing and Urban Development Shaun

Donovan as saying that failure to implement mortgage cram-down "was a missed opportunity. It would have been the right thing to do and it could have helped." Former National Economic Council member Peter Swire agrees that it would have made sense for the administration to push for cram-down early on: "Cram-down, on balance, today, would have been a good idea."[48]

Even the IMF believed stronger "consideration should also be given to allowing mortgage on principal residences to be modified in personal bankruptcy without secured creditors' consent (cram-downs)."[49] In a longer study of several levered-losses episodes, the IMF concluded that "bold household debt restructuring programs . . . can significantly reduce debt repayment burdens and the number of household defaults and foreclosures. Such policies can therefore help avert self-reinforcing cycles of household defaults, further house prices declines, and additional contractions in output."[50]

We can also see the benefits of mortgage write-downs by looking at other types of debt. A research study by Will Dobbie and Jae Song used variation across bankruptcy judges in the willingness to write down non-mortgage debt to see how indebted individuals responded.[51] They found that individuals who received more debt forgiveness saw a decline in five-year mortality risk and significant increases in both earnings and employment. The employment finding is particularly important. It suggests that indebted individuals choose to remain unemployed because creditors immediately garner any potential income that a new job would bring. Recall the story of Manolo Marban in Spain from the last chapter who lamented that he would "be working for the bank for the rest of [his] life." By eliminating the debt hanging over an individual's income prospects, debt forgiveness gives people strong incentives to find a job, which helps the entire economy. The Dobbie and Song study used a clever research design that found a clear causal effect: giving individuals more debt relief causes an increase in their income and employment probability.

The Hazards of Morality

The Santelli rant reflects a belief among many that underwater home owners find themselves in their precarious position because they behaved irresponsibly. Just like the trader on the Chicago Board of Trade floor, many believe that government intervention encourages moral hazard—households must be made to suffer so that they never again borrow so aggressively. As we discussed in chapter 6, many home owners during the boom did indeed treat their homes as ATMs and spent more as a result.

As economists with a strong background in the optimal design of financing arrangements, we have a deep appreciation for moral-hazard concerns. But in this case, we're not dealing with moral hazard. Moral hazard refers to a situation in which a sophisticated individual games a flawed system by taking advantage of a naive counterparty. The classic example of moral hazard is someone driving irresponsibly after getting auto insurance because he knows the insurance company will pay for an accident. If the auto insurance company naively provides unlimited insurance at a cheap price, the driver's moral-hazard problem could become quite severe.

This does not explain what happened during the housing boom. Home owners were not sophisticated individuals who took advantage of naive lenders because they understood house prices were artificially inflated. They weren't counting on a government bailout, and indeed they never received one. In reality, home owners mistakenly believed that house prices would rise forever. Perhaps this was a silly belief, but the image of a sophisticated home owner gaming lenders and the government is wrong. If anything, sophisticated lenders may have taken advantage of naive home owners by convincing them that house prices would continue to rise.

Moral hazard doesn't fit for another reason: the decline in house prices was beyond the control of any home owner in the economy. Imagine a home owner who bought a home in Modesto, California, in 2006 with a 20 percent down payment and never extracted additional home equity. No one would accuse the home owner of "bad behavior." Yet this responsible home owner, through no fault of his own, experienced the complete loss of his home equity from 2006 to 2009 and was pushed way underwater by the 60 percent decline in house prices. How is the loss of wealth the home owner's fault? Why should he be punished? Such massive aggregate shocks are not any one individual's fault and are therefore not well described by the notion of moral hazard.

Moral hazard also does not easily apply to the main policies we advocate, because they are not wholesale taxpayer-funded bailouts of home owners. Instead, we advocate a more even distribution of housing losses between debtors and creditors. Is a more even distribution "unfair"? Remember, it is not a wealth transfer to a guilty party from an innocent one. Both home owners and creditors were culpable in driving the housing boom. The question is how to distribute losses from a bubble gone bad that both helped inflate. Our main argument is that a more even distribution of losses between debtors and creditors is not only fair, but makes more sense from a macroeconomic perspective.

Another argument we often hear is that we are advocating policies that would keep home owners in homes they cannot afford. We disagree. A more aggressive restructuring of household debt may have made it *easier* for home owners to sell homes they could not afford. When a home owner wants to sell his home while underwater on his mortgage, he must sell it for a price less than what he owes the lender. He must therefore bring cash to closing to pay off his lender, cash he most likely does not have. The only other option is default, which is undesirable for many reasons. In this situation, many home owners continued making mortgage payments and living in a home they could not afford. If their debt was restructured so they were no longer underwater, many of these same home owners would have sold and moved.

Moral hazard is a serious issue, but we must also recognize the extreme circumstances of the Great Recession. When a patient is dying of a heart attack, it is not the best time to explain that he should have eaten less red meat. Most agree that some government intervention is necessary when the economy is in free fall. Any government intervention involves redistribution from some individuals to others. Bailouts of financial institutions force innocent taxpayers to bear the burden of irresponsible lending. Fiscal stimulus requires future taxpayers to fund current government expenditure.

So the question is not whether government should intervene when a severe recession strikes. The real question is which intervention is most effective in raising output and reducing unemployment. We outlined the government's urgency to protect the banks in the previous chapter. In this chapter, we discussed the possible alternative of debt forgiveness—a policy that was not pursued by the government. In the Great Recession, the government also relied on fiscal and monetary policy to combat economic weakness. How effective were these policies? Can we rely on a combination of fiscal and monetary policy as an alternative to debt forgiveness? The next chapter explains how fiscal and monetary policy fit into our levered-losses framework.

11: MONETARY AND FISCAL POLICY

In the first four years of the Great Depression, prices and wages fell a remarkable 30 percent. Households had accumulated huge debts, and such rapid deflation devastated the overall economy. Wages fell precipitously, but debt obligations remained the same in dollar terms. So households that already cut back on spending due to high debt were forced to cut back even more. During the Depression, debt and deflation created a deadly mix that amplified the levered-losses forces we've discussed.

Debt and deflation are natural partners in crime. When indebted households cut spending, stores cut prices to boost overall sales. However, this is sustainable only if the firms that lower prices also lower wages to reduce costs. Thus lower demand translates into lower wages, which exacerbates the problem further by increasing households' debt burdens compared to their income. This forces households to cut back on spending even further. And so on.

The great American economist Irving Fisher called this vicious cycle "debt deflation." As he put it in 1933, "I have . . . a strong conviction that these two economic maladies, the debt disease and the price-level disease, are, in the great booms and depressions, more important causes than all others put together."[1] His was a *distributional* argument. Because debt contracts are fixed in dollar terms, deflation makes it more onerous for the borrower to repay his debts. On the other side, the creditor gains from deflation because he can purchase more goods from the same interest payment he receives on his loan. Deflation is a mechanism that transfers purchasing power—or wealth—from debtors to creditors.

So if deflation takes purchasing power away from debtors, does *inflation* help soften the blow by giving purchasing power back to debtors? In principle, yes. An increase in prices and wages makes it easier for borrowers to use their higher wages to pay back their fixed-debt obligations. Likewise, higher prices reduce the value of interest payments to creditors. The higher marginal propensity to consume for debtors means that such a transfer in purchasing power is beneficial for the overall economy—debtors spend out of an increase in purchasing power more than creditors cut spending in response to the same loss. Which brings us to the importance of monetary policy. By the logic above, if monetary policy can prevent deflation and support inflation, it can reduce the ill effects of a debt-driven recession.

During the Great Depression, the Federal Reserve didn't prevent deflation, and it has been roundly criticized. Milton Friedman and Anna Schwartz, for example, in their 1963 classic, *A Monetary History of the United States*, chastised the Fed for keeping the money supply too tight and failing to prevent deflation. On the occasion of Milton Friedman's ninetieth birthday in 2002, Ben Bernanke—a former professor of economics at Princeton and an expert on the Great Depression—publicly pledged: "I would like to say to Milton and Anna: Regarding the Great Depression. You're right, we did it. We're very sorry. But thanks to you, we won't do it again."[2]

Bernanke proved to be a man of his word. When the real test came in 2007 and 2008, the Fed's spigots flowed uninhibited. (See the long list of steps taken by the Fed in chapter 9.) The Fed's aggressive approach indeed helped prevent a repeat of the deflationary spiral of the Great Depression. Still, we did not see higher inflation during the Great Recession, even though it would have lowered the macroeconomic damage of debt. Why didn't the Fed simply inflate away the levered-losses problem?

A Magic Inflation Button?

Unfortunately, no central banker has a magic button they can simply push to create inflation. Preventing deflation is one thing; generating significant inflation is much harder. In fact, when an economy suffers from excessive debt burdens and finds itself at the zero lower bound, the ability of monetary policy to push up prices becomes severely impaired. Even beyond the well-documented limitations imposed by the zero lower bound, the levered-losses problem substantially weakens the power of monetary policy.

To understand why, we must look into the details of how the Federal Reserve operates. The most direct way to get inflation is through a large increase in the amount of currency in circulation. As more money chases the same amount of goods and services, prices and wages must rise. The monetary base of the United States includes both *currency in circulation*—the coins and bills we usually think of as money—and *bank reserves*. Bank reserves are cash held within the banking system, both as currency in bank vaults and as deposits that banks hold with the Federal Reserve.

Bank reserves are not currency in circulation. When the Fed wants to increase the monetary base, it purchases securities (usually U.S. Treasuries) from banks and pays them with bank reserves. In other words, the Fed creates *bank reserves*, not currency in circulation.[3] An increase in bank reserves leads to an increase in currency in circulation only if banks increase lending in response to the increase in reserves. If banks don't lend more—or, equivalently, if borrowers don't borrow more—an increase in bank reserves doesn't affect money in circulation. This is what happened in the Great Recession. The aggressive actions taken by the Fed comprised lending to banks—this increased bank reserves and lowered interbank interest rates, but it had a limited effect on actual lending, and therefore a limited effect on currency in circulation. As shown in chapter 9, bank lending plummeted during the Great Recession—just as bank reserves skyrocketed.

Many readers may be surprised, but it is true: the Federal Reserve does not have direct control over currency in circulation. It does not print *money*; it prints *bank reserves*. Following the Great Depression, a group of prestigious economists, including Irving Fisher, were furious about this lack of control and strongly advocated policies to give full authority to the Fed. They wrote, "[Current policies] give our thousands of commercial banks power to increase or decrease the volume of our circulating medium by increasing or decreasing bank loans and investments. The banks thus exercise what has always, and justly, been considered a prerogative of the sovereign power."[4] The economists were unable implement their policies, however, and the same problem plagued monetary policy in response to the Great Recession seventy years later.

In the context of a levered-losses recession, relying on banks to increase lending severely weakens monetary policy. Remember, in a levered-losses episode, households and even businesses struggle to pay back debt, and banks suffer high default rates. In such a situation, banks don't want to supply more loans, and households don't want additional debt. So just when monetary policy needs more lending to put currency into circulation, natural forces in the economy discourage lending.[5]

We can see just how this happened in the Great Recession by comparing the growth of bank reserves with currency in circulation. In the five months from August 2008 to January 2009, bank reserves increased by ten times—from $90 billion to $900 billion—which reflects the extremely aggressive stance of the Fed. Aggressive monetary policy continued through 2013, with bank reserves over $2 trillion as we write.

Currency in circulation increased, but only by a modest amount compared to the increase in bank reserves. Figure 11.1 illustrates this pattern. Aggressive monetary policy moved bank reserves significantly, but there was only a minor knock-on effect on the currency in circulation. Banks not wanting to lend and households not wanting to borrow limited the effectiveness of monetary policy. The Fed avoided deflation, but there's likely no way it could have generated significant inflation.

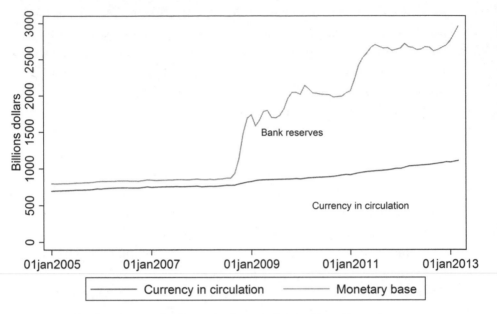

Figure 11.1: The Monetary Base during the Great Recession

The impotence of central bankers during a levered-losses episode is not unique to the Great Recession in the United States. The pattern in figure 11.1 also held in the Great Depression, as pointed out by both Paul Krugman and Peter Temin.[6] And Richard Koo showed that both continental Europe and the United Kingdom during the Great Recession witnessed a similar increase in bank reserves while currency in circulation remained constant. The same holds true for Japan from 1994 on.[7] Central banks fight a levered-losses recession by flooding the banking system with reserves, but nobody wants to lend or borrow. One proposal would be to try even harder to get banks to lend. But we saw the problems with this approach in chapter 9. It doesn't make economic sense for banks to lend into an economy plagued with too much debt. More debt is not the solution to a debt problem.

A better approach would be to allow central banks to directly inject cash into the economy, bypassing the banking system altogether. The most extreme image that comes to mind is the chairman of the Federal Reserve authorizing helicopter drops of cash. The idea of directly injecting cash into the economy may at first seem crazy, but reputable economists and commentators have suggested exactly such a policy during severe economic downturns.[8] Ben Bernanke, only a few years before he was chairman of the Fed, suggested helicopter drops for Japanese central bankers in the 1990s, earning the nickname "Helicopter Ben."[9] *Financial Times* columnist Martin Wolf wrote in February 2013 that "the view that it is never right to respond to a financial crisis with monetary financing of a consciously expanded fiscal deficit—helicopter money, in brief—is wrong. It simply has to be in the toolkit."[10] Willem Buiter used rigorous modeling to show that such helicopter drops would in fact help an economy trapped at the zero lower bound on nominal interest rates.[11] It would be best if the helicopters targeted indebted areas of the country to drop cash. The exercise would have positive effects similar to the debt restructuring we proposed in the previous chapter.

As you may have guessed, dropping cash from helicopters is only an analogy. In reality, the Fed potentially could inject cash by printing money and paying teachers' salaries, for example. However, the problem is that it is against the law for the Fed to print money and hand it out to people. Currency is technically a liability of the government, and the issuance of any government liability is a fiscal action that only the Treasury can undertake. This explains why the Federal Reserve must *exchange* bank reserves for securities. They are not allowed to put currency or bank reserves into circulation without taking a security in return. Moreover, do we believe that central bankers would take such actions even if they had the authority? In most advanced economies, central bankers build their careers on the conservative credentials of inflation busting. It is hard to imagine them happily dropping cash on cities throughout the nation. We'll return to this point later in the chapter.

The Interest-Rate Channel

Increasing the monetary base is not the only way central bankers try to spur economic activity in a crisis. They also lower interest rates that may not be up against the zero lower bound. For example, during the Great Recession and afterward, the Federal Reserve aggressively purchased mortgage-backed securities in order to push down mortgage interest rates facing households. The belief was that cheaper rates on outstanding mortgages and other loans through which households would spend would kick-start the economy.

However, households that normally have the highest marginal propensity to consume out of loans either cannot or do not want to borrow more. Remember, in a levered-losses episode, borrowers experience a massive shock to their wealth. Many of them are underwater on their homes or have very low credit scores as a result of default. Most are desperate to rebuild their balance sheets by saving, and the last thing they want is additional debt. Of those who do want to borrow, most are shut out of the credit market, which in a crisis lends only to those with pristine credit histories.

While the interest rate on thirty-year mortgages went down from 6.5 percent in July 2007 to 3.5 percent in July 2012, banks significantly restricted the range of borrowers who could benefit from the lower rates. As a result, in March 2012, 70 percent of borrowers with a thirty-year fixed-rate mortgage were paying an interest rate of 5 percent or more, despite the fact that market mortgage interest rates were only 3.8 percent.[12]

Indebted home owners couldn't get lower mortgage rates, so monetary policy during and after the Great Recession was much less effective. To refinance an existing mortgage, most banks require that a home owner have substantial equity in their home. But when house prices collapsed, so did home owners' equity. In Arizona, Florida, and Nevada—where more than 50 percent of home owners were underwater—the propensity to refinance was the lowest in the country. Figure 11.2 illustrates this correlation for all states in 2010.

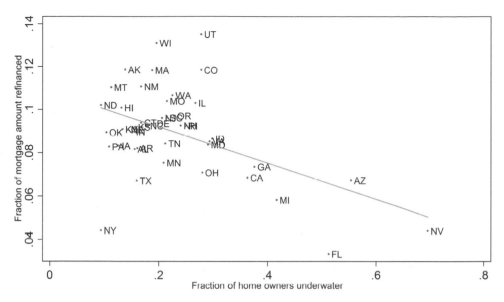

Figure 11.2: Underwater Home Owners and Mortgage Refinancing, 2010

Further, when home owners refinanced their existing mortgages during the Great Recession, they did not take cash out. In fact, the fraction of refinancing in which the home owner took out additional equity was lower in 2012 than at any other point since 1993. Figure 11.3 shows the fraction of all refinancing where a home owner took cash out. During the housing boom it exploded, as home owners aggressively pulled equity out of their homes, and then plummeted from 2008 to 2012, just as the Federal Reserve tried to spur more borrowing with lower interest rates.

During a levered-losses scenario, banks refuse to lend and households avoid borrowing. The same problems that hinder central bankers' attempts to increase currency in circulation also thwart their ability to spur household borrowing. Monetary policy is unable to resuscitate the debt cycle.

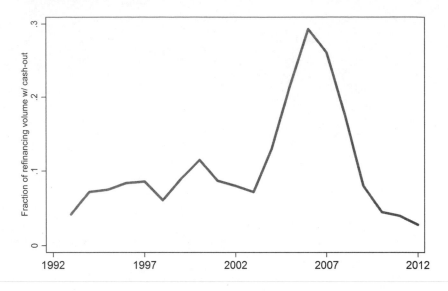

Figure 11.3: Disappearance of Cash-out Refinancings

Inflation Expectations

When central bankers expand bank reserves in a levered-losses re-cession, there is no increase in lending or borrowing, and a severe and long economic slump ensues. But eventually the economy may recover, and if the central bank keeps interest rates very low, banks will resume lending and this will spark inflation. Some argue that if the general public *expects* inflation in the long run, then the economy may benefit even in the short run. According to this view, inflation expectations may be able to generate increased spending even when the economy is up against the zero lower bound. Recall from chapter 4 that interest rates may need to be negative to induce some households to spend more. In other words, to get households to spend, they would need to be *charged* for saving instead of spending. Raising inflation expectations helps get a negative interest rate.

For example, suppose you save $1,000 in a bank account that pays zero interest. If you expect the price of the goods you plan to buy in the future to rise, the future buying power of your $1,000 in the bank declines. In other words, in terms of the real goods you purchase, inflation leads to a *negative* interest rate on your bank deposit. This will encourage you to spend rather than save, thereby increasing aggregate demand. If the Fed can just get you to believe that inflation will eventually emerge, the inflation expectations view holds that this can boost the economy.

The problem with this argument, however, is that it assumes that household spending is very sensitive to changes in real interest rates. While this may be true in normal circumstances, a levered-losses episode may sever the link. In an economy with excessive debt and a collapse in asset values, indebted households are forced to massively cut spending, and they are cut out of credit markets even if they wanted to borrow. As a result, even negative interest rates won't boost spending substantially.

But let us suppose that household spending would respond to higher inflation expectations. A serious problem remains: it is extremely difficult for central banks to create higher inflation expectations in a levered-losses recession. Households will only expect higher inflation if the central banker commits to allowing inflation even when the economy recovers and escapes the zero lower bound on nominal interest rates.

But central bankers' reputations are built on *fighting* inflation. Given this, the general public expects that the central bank will step in to take the reserves out of the system when the economy begins to recover. If central bankers cannot be trusted to allow inflation when the economy recovers, then the economy gets no benefits from higher inflation expectations. As Paul Krugman famously wrote about the Japanese Lost Decade, "Monetary policy will in fact be effective if the central bank can credibly promise to be *irresponsible* . . ." (our emphasis).[13] We would go further. Monetary policy makers would need to commit to being *very* irresponsible to generate inflation expectations in the midst of a levered-losses downturn. When the crash materializes, households sharply reduce spending. In the face of massively depleted demand, the natural re-

action by businesses would be to *cut* prices and wages. This is exactly what happened during the Great Depression. Once again, the
natural forces of the economy move *against* inflation and *toward*
deflation during a severe economic downturn. Monetary policy
fights an uphill battle.

Are central banks willing to act irresponsibly enough to win?
The evidence suggests no. The European Central Bank has been
conservative in its approach, as has the Bank of England. The Federal Reserve has pushed the envelope with aggressive quantitative
easing and conditional guidance language in its statements. But
as former chair of the Council of Economic Advisers Christina
Romer put it, "The truth is that even these moves were pretty small
steps . . . the key fact remains that the Fed has been unwilling to do
a regime shift. And because of that, monetary policy has not been
able to play a decisive role in generating recovery."[14]

Relying on monetary policy to generate inflation through expectations may work beautifully in macroeconomic models. But relying on the irresponsibility of central bankers is a losing strategy. We
cannot count on them to magically fix the debt problem.

What about the Fiscal Alternative?

Unlike "Keynesian" theories, the levered-losses framework we have
developed focuses on the *source* of the demand shock, which leads
naturally to policies that directly attack the problem of excessive
household debt. Nonetheless, government spending during a severe economic downturn helps because it increases aggregate demand. Most economists agree that in normal times government
spending has little effect on the economy, because it crowds out
private spending and because households understand that they
eventually have to pay higher taxes to finance the spending. If anything, government spending may hurt in normal times because
it distorts incentives through taxation. But when frictions like
the zero lower bound keep the economy depressed, government
spending financed with debt can have positive economic effects.

Substantial evidence shows the short-run benefits of fiscal stimulus, especially when the economy is up against the zero lower bound. Emi Nakamura and Jon Steinsson examined the effect on state-level GDP of defense-spending shocks to states over the past fifty years. They found large effects. One dollar of defense spending generated $1.50 of economic output. As they write, "Our estimate provides evidence in favor of models in which demand shocks can have large effects on output."[15] Two other independent studies found positive benefits of the American Recovery and Reinvestment Act passed in 2009. Using variation across states in the funds received from the legislation, both found meaningful effects on jobs.[16]

So fiscal stimulus can help, and efforts to impose austerity in the midst of a levered-losses episode are counterproductive. However, in our view, fiscal stimulus is much less effective than household-debt restructuring when the fundamental problem with the economy is excessive private debt. The most effective policy puts cash into the hands of those who will spend the most of it, and indebted home owners have an extremely high marginal propensity to consume. The greater effectiveness of debt restructuring, as compared to fiscal stimulus, emerges in some of the most influential "Keynesian" models of the Great Recession. For example, Gauti Eggertsson and Paul Krugman wrote an influential theoretical study in which the levered-losses view plays an important role. A main takeaway is that "a rationale for expansionary fiscal policy [emerges] naturally from the model."[17] But in their model, the economy hits the zero lower bound on nominal interest rates because indebted home owners are forced to drastically cut spending. In the context of their model, an immediate restructuring of household debt would help avoid the liquidity trap in the first place by avoiding the sharp drop in demand. Krugman is a strong proponent of household-debt restructuring.[18]

Fiscal stimulus is a clumsy alternative. Unless the fiscal stimulus takes the form of principal forgiveness, it doesn't target the right population.[19] Further, government spending must eventually be paid for by someone through taxes. Unless those taxes fall on creditors in the economy who were responsible for the housing boom, fiscal policy fails to replicate the transfer from creditors to debtors that most effectively boosts aggregate demand. Put another way, the most effective fiscal stimulus would be one in which the government taxes creditors and provides the funds to debtors. But why do we need fiscal stimulus? Mortgage cram-downs in bankruptcy, for example, would accomplish the same goal without getting taxation involved.

Fiscal policy is an attempt to replicate debt restructuring, but it is particularly problematic in the United States, where government revenue is raised from taxing *income*, not *wealth*.[20] The creditors whom the government should tax tend to be the wealthiest people in the economy, which is why they are able to lend to borrowers. But the wealthy do not necessarily have high incomes; similarly, those with high incomes are not necessarily wealthy. For example, a retired investment banker may have no income but high wealth, whereas a young professional couple may have high income but low wealth. Think of the young professional couple just starting their post–graduate school jobs. They have high income but almost no wealth. Their MPC out of income may be very high: they expect a steady stream of high income but need to make large capital investments upfront on things like furnishing their first apartment. Taxing them will hurt the economy. Also, by taxing income, the government distorts incentives for working, perhaps leading one of the professionals in the relationship to stay out of the labor force. All these problems suggest that a tax code that relies on taxing income will be much less effective at solving the levered-losses problem compared to household-debt restructuring.

Finally, debt restructuring preserves incentives in the marketplace. As we argued in chapter 8, every levered-losses disaster is preceded by an asset-price bubble that creditors fuel with easy debt. They bear some responsibility for the ensuing catastrophe, and imposing some losses on them disciplines an actor that helped cause the crisis in the first place. Taxpayers are rightfully indignant when asked to pay for the mistakes of others, and forcing creditors to bear losses should be more politically acceptable than most forms of fiscal stimulus. Economist Hans-Werner Sinn expressed this exactly when writing with indignation on the crisis in Europe, where German taxpayers were being asked to bail out banks. As he put it, "A bailout doesn't make economic sense, and would likely make the situation worse. Such schemes violate the liability principle, one of the constituting principles of a market economy, which holds that it is the creditors' responsibility to choose their debtors. If debtors cannot repay, creditors should bear the losses."[21]

Political Paralysis

In the last three chapters, we've evaluated the potential policies that governments may implement when a levered-losses crisis hits. Saving the banks at any cost is counterproductive. Monetary policy and fiscal policy help, but are inferior to a direct attack on household debt, which is after all the main problem. Restructuring debt will most effectively boost an ailing economy.

While it is useful to discuss which policies are best when a crisis hits, such a discussion ignores the gargantuan elephant in the room: if we have learned anything about politics in the past few years, we should know that partisan conflict poisons governments during severe economic contractions. When it is needed most, policy is impotent. For example, the electorate in the United States became extremely polarized during the Great Recession. The emergence of groups like the Tea Party movement and Occupy Wall Street exemplify a broader trend: during the heart of the Great Recession, the fraction of the population in the United States calling themselves moderate plummeted.[22]

In research with Francesco Trebbi, we show that the political polarization in the United States over the past seven years was the rule, not the exception.[23] More specifically, we examined political polarization in the aftermath of financial crises from 1981 to 2008 in seventy countries.[24] When a crisis materializes, the fraction of the population calling themselves centrists falls sharply. In its place is a large increase in the share of extremists, on both the left and the right.

In turn, financial crises move political systems toward more fragmented legislatures and political scenarios. Governments are less able to form viable coalitions, and political disintegration becomes the norm. Even if every economist in the world agreed on the correct policies, we would not be able to count on governments to enact them. The debt-ceiling debacle of the summer of 2011, the sequestration of 2013, the failure of the U.S. government to implement any meaningful legislation in the past few years—these are not exceptions, but instead represent how the government becomes impotent when the economy collapses. We cannot rely on officials to nimbly implement the right policies when a levered-losses recession strikes. We must somehow have mechanisms in place that automatically help the economy respond when asset prices collapse.

Debt is a horrible instrument because of its *inflexibility*: it requires intervention after the fact to help more equally distribute the losses associated with a crash. Because of political polarization, such intervention is unlikely. And the time, energy, and resources wasted in fighting over debt restructuring can be costly. In the next chapter, we argue that the vicious levered-losses cycle can be broken only if we fundamentally alter the way in which households finance themselves. We must have mechanisms in place that help us avoid levered-losses crises in the first place. We can enjoy the fruits of the financial system only if we move away from a system so addictively reliant on debt.

12: SHARING

The college graduating class of 2010 had little time to celebrate their freshly minted diplomas. The severe recession smacked them with the harsh reality of looking for a job in a horrible labor market. For college graduates at the time, the unemployment rate was over 10 percent.[1] When they entered college in 2006, none of them could have predicted such a disastrous situation. Since 1989, the unemployment rate for college graduates had never exceeded 8 percent.

The bleak jobs picture threatened the livelihood of recent graduates for another reason: many left college saddled with enormous student-debt burdens. Driven by the allure of a decent salary with a college degree, Americans borrowed to go to school. Outstanding student debt doubled from 2005 to 2010, and by 2012 total student debt in the U.S. economy surpassed $1 trillion.[2] The Department of Education estimated that two-thirds of bachelor's degree recipients borrowed money from either the government or private lenders.[3]

Unfortunately for the 2010 graduates, debt contracts don't care what the labor market looks like when you graduate. Regardless of whether a graduate can find a well-paying job, they demand payment. Student debt is especially pernicious in this regard because it cannot be discharged in bankruptcy. And the government can garnish your wages or take part of your tax refund or Social Security payments to ensure that they get paid on federal loans.[4]

The combination of unemployment and the overhang of student

debt hampered demand just when the economy needed it most. Recent college graduates with high student debt delayed major purchases, and many were forced to move back in with their parents.[5] As Andrew Martin and Andrew Lehren of the *New York Times* put it, "Growing student debt hangs over the economic recovery like a dark cloud for a generation of college graduates and indebted dropouts."[6] Many reconsidered the benefits of college altogether. Ezra Kazee, an unemployed college graduate with $29,000 of student debt, was interviewed for a story on student-loan burdens. "You often hear the quote that you can't put a price on ignorance," he said. "But with the way higher education is going, ignorance is looking more and more affordable every day."[7]

The Risk-Sharing Principle

The student debt debacle is another example of the financial system failing us. Despite the high cost of a college degree, most economists agree that it is valuable because of the wage premium it commands. Yet young Americans increasingly recognize that student debt unfairly forces them to bear a large amount of aggregate economic risk. Debt protects the lender even if the job market deteriorates, but graduates are forced to cobble money together to pay down the loan. Forcing young Americans to bear this risk makes no economic sense. College graduates were thrown into dire circumstances just because they happened to be born in 1988, twenty-two years before the most disastrous labor market in recent history. Why should they be punished for that? Rather than facilitate the acquisition of valuable knowledge, a financial system built on debt increasingly discourages college aspirations.

Both student debt and mortgages illustrate a broader principle. If we're going to fix the financial system—if we are to avoid the painful boom-and-bust episodes that are becoming all too frequent—we must address the key problem: the inflexibility of debt contracts. When someone finances the purchase of a home or a college education, the contract they sign must allow for some sharing of the downside risk. The contract must be made contingent on economic outcomes so that the financial system helps us. It must resemble *equity* more than *debt*.[8]

This principle can be seen easily in the context of education. Student loans should be made contingent on measures of the job market at the time the student graduates. For example, in both Australia and the United Kingdom, students pay only a fixed percentage of their income to pay down student loans. If the student cannot find a job, she pays nothing on her student loan. For reasons we will discuss, we believe a better system would make the loan payment contingent on a broader measure of the labor market rather than the individual's income. But the principle is clear: recent graduates should be protected if they face a dismal job market upon completing their degrees.[9] In return, they should compensate the lender more if they do well.

The disadvantage of debt in the context of student loans is not a radical leftist idea. Even Milton Friedman recognized problems with student debt. As he put it, "A further complication is introduced by the inappropriateness of fixed money loans to finance investment in training. Such investment necessarily involves much risk. The average expected return may be high, but there is wide variation about the average. Death and physical incapacity is one obvious source of variation but probably much less important than differences in ability, energy, and good fortune."[10] Friedman's proposal was similar to ours: he believed that student-loan financing should be more "equity-like," where payments were automatically reduced if the student graduates into a weak job environment.

Making financial contracts in general more equity-like means better risk sharing for the entire economy. When house prices rise, both the lender and borrower would benefit. Likewise, when house prices crash, both would share the burden. This is not about forcing lenders to unfairly bear only downside risk. This is about promoting contracts in which the financial system gets both the benefit of the upside and bears some cost on the downside.

Financial contracts that share more of the risk would help avoid bubbles and make their crashes less severe. Recall from chapter 8 how debt facilitates bubbles by convincing lenders that their money is safe, and how this leads them to lend to optimists who bid prices higher and higher. If lenders were forced to take losses when the bubble pops, they would be less likely to lend into the bubble in the first place. They would be less likely to be lulled into the false sense of security that debt dangerously offers. Charles Kindleberger saw time and time again that bubbles were driven by investors' believing that the securities they held were as safe as money. We must break this cycle.

We have also shown that when borrowers are forced to bear the entire brunt of the crash in asset prices, the levered-losses cycle kicks in and a very severe recession ensues. If financial contracts more equally imposed losses on both borrowers and lenders, then the economy would avoid the levered-losses trap in the first place. This would force wealthy lenders with deep pockets to bear more of the pain if a crash materializes. But their spending would be less affected, and the initial demand shock to the economy would be much smaller. In the context of housing, a more equal sharing of losses would also help avoid the painful cycle of foreclosures. If financial contracts were structured appropriately, we could avoid foreclosure crises entirely.

In chapter 10, we advocated policies that would help restructure household debt when a crash materializes. But intervening after the fact requires political will and popular support, both of which are absent during a severe recession. The contingent contracts we propose here would automatically accomplish many of these goals. And they would preserve incentives because all parties would understand what they were signing up for. In the next section, we propose a specific mortgage contract that includes these features, which we call the *shared-responsibility mortgage*. As we will demonstrate, had such mortgages been in place when house prices collapsed, the Great Recession in the United States would not have been "Great" at all. It would have been a garden-variety downturn with many fewer jobs lost.

Shared-Responsibility Mortgages

As we discussed in chapter 2, a standard mortgage contract forces the borrower to bear the full burden of a decline in house prices until his equity is completely wiped out. A shared-responsibility mortgage (SRM) has two important differences: (1) the lender offers *downside protection* to the borrower, and (2) the borrower gives up *5 percent capital gain* to the lender on the upside.[11] We go through a simple example here to see how it works.

Consider a home owner, Jane. She uses a $20,000 down payment to buy a house worth $100,000, leaving her with a mortgage of $80,000. Suppose the value of her house drops to $70,000. In a standard thirty-year fixed-rate mortgage contract, Jane loses all of her home equity, which was probably most of her savings. She faces two choices at this point. She can give the keys of the house back to the bank, or she can continue making her mortgage payment despite these payments not adding a dime to her equity in the house. Neither of these options is particularly attractive for Jane. However, the core point of the levered-losses framework is that *both of these options are terrible for the rest of us*. The decline in home value leads Jane to pull back massively on spending, and this pullback will be exacerbated if she continues to pay her mortgage. If she allows the bank to foreclose, house prices are pushed down further, accelerating the vicious cycle of lost wealth.

How could a shared-responsibility mortgage help? If house prices remain the same or rise, the interest payment on Jane's SRM would remain the same. For example, if the current thirty-year mortgage rate were 5 percent, then Jane would be required to make the same mortgage payment of $5,204 to her lender every year under the SRM, just as under the typical fixed-rate mortgage.[12] Also like a fixed-rate mortgage, a portion of Jane's $5,204 payment will go toward interest and the remainder toward principal. The amortization schedule, the rate at which her mortgage balance goes down over the thirty years, remains exactly the same in an SRM as in a standard fixed-rate mortgage.

The key difference between the SRM and typical mortgage is that the SRM provides downside protection to Jane in case the value of her home goes down from the value when she purchased it. This is accomplished by linking Jane's mortgage-payment schedule to her local house-price index. Linking the downside protection to Jane's local house-price index instead of just her home avoids the possibility of Jane deliberately neglecting her home to lower her mortgage payments.[13] Another benefit of using a local house-price index is its widespread availability. A number of firms—like Core-Logic, Zillow, Fiserv Case-Shiller-Weiss, and the Federal Housing Finance Agency Local—produce these indexes, many of them at the zip-code level. Further credibility could be added to these indices by adopting a commonly accepted framework for constructing them, and a government or industry watchdog could be collectively responsible for ensuring their authenticity. Making payments contingent on public indices is nothing new. For example, many countries have adopted payments that are linked to some index of inflation. The U.S. government itself issues inflation-indexed government bonds for which interest payments fluctuate depending on an inflation index.

The downside-protection provision works by proportionately reducing Jane's mortgage payment in case the housing index falls below the level it was when Jane purchased her property. For example, if her local house-price index is 100 when she buys the home, and falls by 30 percent by the end of her first year of ownership, Jane's mortgage payment in her second year would decline 30 percent, to $3,643. While Jane's mortgage payment declines by 30 percent in the example above, her amortization schedule would remain the same. As a result, even though she will make a lower payment, her mortgage balance goes down according to the original formula. This in effect means that Jane is given an automatic principal reduction when house prices in her area fall below her purchasing level. In our specific example, if Jane's house-price index remains at 70 for the remaining twenty-nine years of her mortgage, she will have received a 30 percent forgiveness in principal by the end of her thirty years.

However, on average, house prices are expected to grow. It is therefore likely that after falling to 70, Jane's house-price index will rise again and at some point will surpass the original mark of 100. As the local house-price index gradually recovers, Jane's mortgage payments will also gradually increase. Once her local house-price index crosses 100, her mortgage payment will once again revert to the full payment of $5,204.

Interest rates tend to fall during recessions. As a result, existing adjustable rate mortgages offer some protection by automatically lowering the interest rate when the economy sputters. But the downside protection of SRMs is much more significant. Not only does Jane experience a lower interest payment, but she also experiences a decline in the principal balance of the mortgage, which leaves her with some equity in the home.

This downside protection comes at the expense of the lender. So the lender will need to charge a higher upfront interest rate to compensate for the downside risk. How large is the upfront cost? The cost of providing downside protection depends on expected house-price growth and house-price volatility. If house prices typically grow at a brisk pace, then the cost of providing the downside protection is low. On the other hand, if house prices are very volatile, then there is a higher chance that at some point they might drop below the purchase level for the mortgage. In this case, the cost of the protection would be high.

Using a standard financial formula, one can calculate the cost of providing downside protection for given house-price growth and volatility. House prices in the United States have historically grown at an annual rate of 3.7 percent, with a standard deviation of 8.3 percent. These numbers imply that lenders will charge about 1.4 percent of the initial mortgage amount as downside protection fee from the borrower. However, we can eliminate this extra charge by giving the lender a small share in the upside as well. In particular, an SRM should also provide the lender with a 5 percent share of the capital gain whenever Jane sells or refinances her house. The 5 percent capital-gain rule is a small charge for Jane, especially considering that capital gains on owner-occupied housing are otherwise tax-free. Jane therefore gets to keep 95 percent of her home's capital gain.

The lender does not have to worry about when Jane chooses to sell her house. As long as the lender issues a diverse set of mortgages, it will receive a steady stream of capital gain payments. In particular, 4 to 5 percent of the existing housing stock is sold every year. We can once again use a financial formula to calculate the benefit to the lender from the capital-gains provision. Historical average house-price growth implies that a 5 percent capital-gain rule more than compensates the lender for the downside protection. On net the lender comes out ahead by 0.81 percent of the initial mortgage amount. The costs of SRMs are even lower if one takes into account the reduction in house-price volatility as a result of the risk-sharing. If SRMs are adopted at a large scale in the United States, house-price volatility—particularly the probability of a big collapse—is likely to go down. We discuss the reasons for this decline in more detail in the next section.

Quantifying the Benefits of SRMs

SRMs provide an important mechanism needed to solve the levered-losses problem. The downside protection to borrowers will help stave off dramatic declines in demand, and the shared capital gains on the upside will compensate lenders. But what would be the exact benefits of SRMs in terms of spending and jobs? An advantage of our data-intensive approach is that we can offer a realistic estimate. In what follows, we ask the following question: How bad would the Great Recession have been had all home owners had SRMs instead of standard mortgages?

The immediate consequence of SRMs in the face of house-price declines is that the wealth of low to middle net-worth Americans would have been protected. Recall from chapter 2 how low net-worth indebted households were hit hardest by the housing collapse in the Great Recession. The downside protection in SRMs would have guaranteed everyone at least the same percentage of home equity as they had had when they initially purchased the home.

For example, under an SRM, if a house with an $80,000 mortgage drops in value from $100,000 to $70,000, then the mortgage interest payment also drops by 30 percent, which means the mortgage value drops by 30 percent (if house prices are expected to remain low). As a result, the new mortgage value would be $56,000. The home owner retains $14,000 of equity in a $70,000 home, which is 20 percent. Notice that the home owner bears a loss; their home equity declines from $20,000 to $14,000. But the loss is far smaller than with a standard debt contract, with which their full $20,000 would have been lost. As a result, the United States would have been protected from the large increase in wealth inequality that it witnessed between 2006 and 2009.

But the advantages of SRMs go much further. They would have benefited *everyone* by protecting the entire economy against foreclosures and the sharp drop in aggregate spending. A primary economic benefit of SRMs would have come from avoiding foreclosures. The downside protection embedded in SRMs implies that the loan-to-value (LTV) ratio would never have gone higher than what it was at origination. For example, if a home owner buys a home with a 20 percent down payment, he is guaranteed to have at least a 20 percent equity in the house regardless of future house-price movements.

If all mortgages in the economy had been structured as SRMs, we would never have had so many home owners underwater. Even if someone could not have afforded to make monthly payments anymore, they would not have gone into foreclosure. Since they had equity in the house, they would have been better off selling the house and pocketing the home equity. SRMs would have eliminated the incidence of a large-scale foreclosure crisis. Interestingly, this feature of SRMs also would have reduced the magnitude of the housing crisis itself. The prevention of foreclosures would have led to a smaller fall in house prices between 2006 and 2009.

In the research with Francesco Trebbi that we discussed in chapter 2, we quantified the effect of foreclosures on house prices. Our analysis revealed that house prices fell by 1.9 percentage points for every 1 percent of home owners who went into foreclosure between 2007 and 2009. SRMs would have prevented most of the 5.1 percent of houses that went into foreclosure and would have reduced the fall in house prices by 9.7 percentage points between 2007 and 2009. Actual house prices fell by 21 percentage points over this period. So by preventing foreclosures, SRMs could possibly have saved a staggering 46 percent of total housing-wealth loss—or $2.5 trillion.

In turn, ameliorating the decline in housing wealth would have had two positive knock-on effects on the economy: higher household spending and fewer job losses. Chapter 3 discussed the impact of reduced housing wealth on household spending. The results show that households cut back six cents of spending in 2006–2009 for every dollar of housing wealth lost. Using this estimate, an increase of $2.5 trillion in housing wealth would have translated into $150 billion of additional household spending.

There also would have been an additional but subtle impact of SRMs on overall spending. Chapter 3 also demonstrated that households with low wealth and high leverage have a higher marginal propensity to consume. SRMs would have helped cushion the blow of a decline in housing wealth by passing some of the losses on to lenders, who have a significantly smaller marginal propensity to spend. Such a transfer of wealth would have led to an overall increase in consumer spending. How much? In the SRM scenario, we estimate housing wealth would have fallen by $3 trillion, or $2.5 trillion less than the actual decline of $5.5 trillion between 2006 and 2009. Alternatively, housing wealth would have fallen only 55 percent of the actual decline experienced between 2006 and 2009.

Since creditors would have shared the downside risk, some of this loss would have been transferred to them from borrowers. We can estimate the impact on creditors using zip-code data on the actual decline in home value and the average loan-to-value ratio for home owners. In the alternative scenario with SRMs, we assign 55 percent of the actual decline in home values to each zip code. We also conservatively assume that borrowers made just a 10 percent down payment on their mortgages. Through the downside protection of SRMs, borrowers who put a 10 percent down payment toward their mortgages would still have kept 10 percent of the equity of the home. A significant number of mortgages were originated with a down payment higher than 10 percent, but we're using 10 percent as a conservative estimate of the equity that borrowers had in their houses. Through the SRMs, no one's equity would have fallen below 10 percent of the value of their house, and their loan-to-value ratio would not have exceeded 90 percent.

The guarantee that the LTV ratio cannot exceed 90 percent tells us how much of the mortgage amount would have needed to be forgiven. That is, it tells us how much of the housing wealth loss would have been passed on to the lender on the SRM. We estimate that about 4.3 percent of single-family outstanding mortgages would have been written down under the downside protection provided by SRMs. Since there was $10.5 trillion in single-family mortgages at the end of 2006, this would have translated into a $451 billion wealth transfer from creditors to borrowers.[14] The wealth transfer translates into a financial loss for lenders and a net housing-wealth gain for borrowers.

Proponents of the banking view might respond that $451 billion of losses on the financial sector would do extreme damage to the economy. However, as we have argued, the idea that financial firms should never take losses is indefensible. They are in the business of taking risk. Also, in a world with SRMs, it is likely that investors who hold them would not be so levered themselves. We seek to encourage an entire financial system more equity-dependent and therefore able to absorb losses.

The estimated marginal propensity to spend out of financial wealth is negligible, while the marginal propensity to consume out of housing wealth for levered, underwater home owners is very high. We estimate that the MPC for underwater home owners is about twice the average MPC.[15] Using a gain of $0.12 in spending per dollar of wealth transferred to borrowers, we arrive at a spending gain of $54 billion for the $451 billion in wealth transferred to borrowers in the SRM scenario.

Overall, a world with SRM mortgages as of 2006 would have seen $150 billion in extra spending from higher housing wealth and $54 billion in extra spending from the transfer of wealth from low MPC lenders to high MPC borrowers. The total increase in aggregate spending would have been $204 billion, which represents substantial stimulus to the overall economy. To put things in perspective, the government stimulus program of 2009 added $550 billion of additional government spending in the short run. The SRM regime would have provided an automatic stimulus that is almost half the government stimulus program—without any increase in government debt.

Preventing Job Loss

Another key advantage of SRMs is that by shoring up aggregate demand in the worst part of the recession, they would have protected jobs as well. We can use the results from chapter 5 to estimate how many jobs would have been saved due to the direct boost in demand from SRMs. The decline in spending between 2006 and 2009 compared to the long-run trend for the United States was $870 billion, and we showed that 4 million of the jobs lost were a direct result of this spending decline. If SRMs would have led to an improvement in consumer spending of $204 billion, then that would have translated to almost 1 million fewer jobs lost between 2006 and 2009.

However, the calculation above is incomplete, since each saved job further contributes toward overall spending, thereby creating a virtuous cycle that augments the original spending increase. The result is what economists call a "multiplier effect." The question of a spending multiplier has received a lot of attention in economics in the context of the *government-spending multiplier*, which measures the extent to which government spending boosts economic output over and above the direct impact of the increase in government spending. Some of the most careful work in this literature comes from Emi Nakamura and Jon Steinsson of Columbia University, who estimate a government spending multiplier of 1.5 on average. However, they estimate that the multiplier is significantly larger— between 3.5 and 4.5—during periods of high unemployment, such as 2007–2009.[16]

That spending multiplier refers to an increase in government spending financed by an increase in future tax revenues. However, the spending boost under the SRM regime would not have been accompanied by expectations of higher taxes. It would have been driven by an increase in private spending. As such, the spending multiplier due to SRMs could have been potentially larger than the government-spending multiplier. Regardless of the exact size of the multiplier, SRMs would have substantially mitigated the severity of the recession. If we use a spending multiplier of 2, then the spending decline would have been only $460 billion instead of $870 billion and 2 million jobs would have been saved. If we use a spending multiplier of 4, the recession would have been almost completely avoided.

Additional Benefits

The benefits of SRMs extend beyond the immediate economic gains. In particular, SRMs would also help prevent bubbles. The downside protection in SRMs would lead lenders to worry about future movements in house prices. If house prices plummet in the near future, then more recently issued mortgages would generate the greatest loss for the lender. The lender would have to be very mindful about potential "froth" in local housing markets, especially for newly originated mortgages. If lenders fear that the market might be in a bubble, they would raise interest rates for new mortgages in order to cover the cost of the increased likelihood of loss. SRMs would therefore provide an automatic market-based "lean against the wind."

Another advantage is that home owners would have to think carefully before doing cash-out refinancing. If home owners refinance in a booming housing market to take extra cash out of their home equity, they would need to pay 5 percent of their net capital gain to the existing lender first. This would be a useful discipline on borrowers, especially in light of evidence that many home owners excessively binged on debt as cash-out refinancing became easier.

Why Don't We See SRMs?

The government provides large tax subsidies to debt financing, and this encourages a financial system overly reliant on debt contracts. In particular, interest payments on debt are tax deductible. The government thus *pushes* the financial system toward debt financing, even though debt financing has horrible consequences for the economy. The mortgage market in particular is dominated by the government and distorted by its tax policy. The most dominant players in the mortgage market are Freddie Mac and Fannie Mae. They decide which mortgage contract is going to dominate the mortgage market, and the rest of the market follows. For example, the thirty-year fixed-interest-rate mortgages were introduced by the government-sponsored enterprises (GSEs) and are rather unique to the United States.[17]

The importance of government in determining the financial contracts that households use is evident in the United Kingdom. In 2013 the United Kingdom government launched the "Help to Buy" program, which provided what David Miles calls an "equity loan." If a household provides a 5 percent down payment and obtains a 75 percent first mortgage, the government provides a 20 percent equity loan, where the value of the loan is fixed at 20 percent of the home value. As a result, if the home falls in value, so does the principal balance on the equity loan. The equity loan in our view is not as desirable as SRMs because of the presence of the first mortgage and more limited risk-sharing if house prices fall. Home owners in the "Help to Buy" program can still go underwater if their house price falls significantly, and the combination of the first mortgage with the equity loan likely inflates house prices. But, as David Miles shows through a series of calculations, the Great Recession in the United Kingdom would have been far less severe had they been in place. The program has proved immensely popular with very high volume of equity loan issuance, which shows how government choices dictate what financial contracts prevail in the marketplace.[18]

Tax policy is another factor that limits innovation in the mortgage industry. The home-owner mortgage-interest deduction encourages home owners to borrow using traditional mortgage contracts. The SRM contract—because of its risk-sharing qualities—would likely not qualify as a "debt instrument" and would therefore not have the same preferential tax treatment as standard mortgages. In fact, the IRS only gives the deduction if the party obtaining the financing—a home owner or shareholders of a corporation—is "subordinate to the rights of general creditors."[19] To get the tax advantage, a home owner must bear the first losses when house prices fall.

We can't really know whether something like shared-responsibility mortgages would emerge organically if the government didn't so strongly support standard mortgages. But the bias of current government policy is important. It means we cannot claim that the absence of SRMs in the marketplace is evidence of their ineffectiveness.

But Debt Is So Cheap!

Moving beyond the mortgage market, the financial system in general relies so heavily on debt because it allows those who want financing—like people buying a home, banks raising financing for loans, or companies building new plants—to get funds at a low cost. Moving away from a debt-based financial system, some argue, would hurt the economy because it would raise the cost of financing.

Debt is cheap because the government massively subsidizes its use. We've discussed the interest-expense tax deduction, but the subsidies are ubiquitous. The entire financial system is based on explicit or implicit government guarantees of the debt of financial intermediaries. Deposit insurance encourages banks to have substantial short-term debt (deposits) in their capital structure. Implicit subsidies to debt financing encourage financial institutions—especially the large ones—to finance themselves almost exclusively with debt. Debt may look cheap to private parties, but the associated expenses are borne by others—taxpayers. And we shouldn't be surprised that financial intermediaries, who are themselves incentivized to use so much inflexible debt financing, would lend to households using the same inflexible debt contracts.

Further, as we have argued throughout the book, debt financing has harmful side effects that are not borne by the parties in a contract—or negative externalities. These include the fire sale of assets below market prices (like foreclosures) and massive aggregate demand shocks (a lot of people cutting back spending) that throw the economy into recession. These large negative externalities are borne by the entire economy, even though debt financing may look cheap to individual parties.

In our view, the massive subsidies to debt financing explain why our financial system is so addicted to it. But some economists argue that debt is an optimal contract for other reasons, and that this explains why it is so cheap. One explanation is that it solves a costly moral hazard. For example, a student loan that demands repayment regardless of the graduating student's future income encourages the student to work diligently toward the highest-paying job possible. In contrast, if the student-loan payment depended on the student's income, the student would have a weaker incentive to find a high-paying job. Why work hard when the bank gets some of my income, and there are no penalties for not working?

When it comes to outcomes that an individual can't control, however, the argument doesn't hold water. A student can control how hard she works in school, but she cannot control what the labor market looks like when she graduates from college. The equity-like contracts we propose here, such as SRMs, would be contingent on a measure of risk that the individual cannot control. In the case of the SRM, the contract would provide downside protection linked to a local house-price index, not the exact house of the owner. For student loans, the contract would require a lower interest payment if the job market deteriorates, not the income of the individual. Contracts that are contingent on risks beyond the control of the individual completely avoid the moral-hazard problem while providing the insurance a borrower needs.

Another common argument for why debt is cheap is that investors demand super-safe assets. In other words, investors are willing to pay a premium for assets that never change in value. Such assets can only be created if the borrower bears all the risk. If equity-like contracts become more dominant, then investors who desire super-safe assets will demand a very large premium to hold them.

But why should investors be unwilling to take risks as long as they are guaranteed a high expected return? Investors are the wealthiest households in the economy, and therefore the sector that should be most willing to bear risk as long as they are properly compensated. We readily admit that there is substantial evidence that investors show an extreme desire to hold what appear to be super-safe assets. But this is likely driven by the same government subsidies to debt financing we have already mentioned. For example, when the financial crisis peaked in September 2008, the U.S. Treasury stepped in to guarantee money-market funds. Now all investors know that money-market funds enjoy an implicit guarantee from the government. Their "desire" to put cash into a money-market fund is not some primitive preference. They are simply responding to a government subsidy.

Also, even if investors do exhibit innate preferences for super-safe assets, the government should directly cater to the demand, not the private sector. The closest thing most economies have to a truly super-safe asset is government debt. If the private sector demands super-safe assets, let the government supply it.[20] As discussed in chapter 7, relying on the private sector for super-safe assets has toxic consequences, and those assets are almost never super-safe. Research by Annette Vissing-Jorgensen and Arvind Krishnamurthy highlights how financial crises are preceded by the banking sector trying to produce super-safe assets when short-term government debt is in short supply. The banking sector's attempt at supplying riskless assets inevitably fails, leading to a financial crisis.[21]

Sharing Risk More Broadly

The risk-sharing principle underlying SRMs applies in many other contexts. For example, during the Great Recession, countries in Europe with particularly high debt burdens, such as Ireland and Spain, suffered a much worse recession than countries that had been lending to them, such as Germany. Why? Partly because of inflexible debt contracts, which forced losses on debtor countries while creditor countries remained protected. The levered-losses framework applies directly to the international system just as it does within the United States.

The debt that a country issues is called sovereign debt, and it has the unfortunate catch that the amount owed does not change even if the country experiences a very severe recession. Even if the economy plummets and unemployment rises above 25 percent, as it has in Spain, the same interest payments on sovereign debt must be paid. A country with debt written in its own currency can reduce the real value of the interest payments by inflating, but countries that had adopted the euro did not have such an option. One proposal is for countries to leave the euro and revert to their own currency. However, given that leaving the euro would lead to default on all euro-denominated debt, an exit could destroy an economy.

In a world of more flexible sovereign financing, such a dramatic course of action would be unnecessary. Mark Kamstra and Robert Shiller have proposed sovereign bonds where the coupon payment—the regular payment that countries make to investors—is linked to the nominal GDP of the country.[22] Such a bond is more equity-like because the investor experiences profits that vary with the fortune of the country, much like an equity holder receives higher or lower dividends depending on earnings of a corporation. In the case of Spain, such financing would act as an *automatic stabilizer*: that is, payments on the bonds would immediately fall when the Spanish economy collapsed, providing some relief to Spaniards.

Kenneth Rogoff, one of the world's leading experts on financial crises, blames sovereign financial crises squarely on the inflexibility of debt contracts. As he notes, "If [advanced economy] governments stood back and asked themselves how to channel a much larger share of the imbalances into equity-like instruments, the global financial system that emerged might be a lot more robust than the crisis-prone system we have now."[23]

There are no doubt complications that arise with such instruments. Should the payments be linked to GDP growth or the level of GDP? How can we ensure that the country doesn't manipulate the GDP numbers to lower their coupon? But these complications should not cloud the overarching goal: to make the international financial system one that more efficiently shares macroeconomic risk instead of inefficiently concentrating it on the most vulnerable countries.

The banking system also needs more risk-sharing, something Anat Admati and Martin Hellwig have articulated.[24] They call for regulators to require more equity financing at financial institutions, which would help insulate the financial system from the horrible shocks we have seen in the recent past. If the banking system was funded with more equity, then banks would not be forced to default on debt when their assets fell. More equity would help prevent banking panics and make it less necessary for central bankers to intervene.

A Financial System that Works for Us

Many of the proposals we are making may sound radical. This is because the financial system is so far from where it should be. As it currently stands, the financial system forces all the risk on the households that can least afford to bear it. Investors look to the financial system to capture government subsidies to debt. Many are lulled into a false sense of security that they are holding super-safe assets, thereby fueling unsustainable bubbles. The financial system is associated with frequent boom-and-bust cycles, leaving everyone worse off. The financial system is earning a higher and higher fraction of our national income, but many Americans don't trust it.

Our proposals bring the financial system closer to what it should ideally look like. Households should use the financial system to share the risk associated with purchasing a home or investing in education. Investors should look to the financial system not to exploit government subsidies, but to take some risk to earn a legitimate return. The financial system should facilitate a growing but stable economy.

The culprit is debt, and the solution is straightforward: The financial system should adopt more equity-like contracts that are made contingent on risks outside the control of households. Investors should earn a return for bearing those risks, and households should be protected when those risks materialize. The government should stop subsidizing the use of inflexible debt contracts, both in the banking and household sectors.

While the solution in principle seems clear, we have no illusion about the challenges of moving toward it. As it currently stands, the financial system benefits very few people, and those few have a vested interest in staving off any reform that could move us away from debt financing. However, we cannot continue down the road of unsustainable debt binges and painful crashes. We must change course to stabilize the world economy. In this book, we have tried to provide an intellectual framework, backed by a plethora of evidence, that can serve as a template of reform. We may not have the specifics exactly right, but we are confident that the general principle of more equity-like financing can help avoid painful recessions and nurture sustainable economic growth.

ACKNOWLEDGMENTS

The research underlying this book was conducted over more than half a decade. Countless colleagues, seminar participants, discussants, and referees contributed to our ideas. We would like to first acknowledge the stimulating intellectual environment of the universities that have employed us over this period: Princeton University, the University of California, Berkeley, and the University of Chicago Booth School of Business. For funding our research, we are very grateful to the Fama-Miller Center at Chicago Booth, the Fisher Center for Real Estate and Urban Economics at UC Berkeley, the Initiative on Global Markets at Chicago Booth, the Julis-Rabinowitz Center for Public Policy and Finance at Princeton, and the National Science Foundation.

Our gratitude also goes out to Kamalesh Rao and Francesco Trebbi, who were our invaluable coauthors on some of the work summarized in this book. Dylan Hall provided excellent research assistance, and his thorough reading greatly improved the book. Comments from Lord Adair Turner, Hal Weitzman, and two anonymous reviewers were extremely helpful. We also thank Sarah Niemann, who provided excellent administrative assistance.

Joe Jackson, our editor at the University of Chicago Press, has been a fantastic adviser throughout, helping us extract from our academic research readable and hopefully enjoyable prose. We also thank Carrie Olivia Adams and the rest of the University of Chicago Press team who made this book a reality.

The book and the research underlying it would not have been possible without the strong support of our families, who somehow put up with our constant absentminded-professorial habits. We dedicate this book to our parents and spouses.

Atif is not eloquent enough to be able to put in words how much he appreciates his parents' love, affection, and innumerable sacrifices. He is also immensely fortunate to have as supportive a life partner as Ayesha Aftab.

Amir thanks Saima Abedin Sufi for her unflinching love and support. She has played the instrumental role in his professional success. He also thanks his parents for always being there to guide him through life's most challenging times.

Last but certainly not least, we thank our children for providing a wonderful distraction from our research while simultaneously providing us a reason to do the research in the first place: to hopefully make the world a better place for future generations.

NOTES

CHAPTER ONE

1. The information on northern Indiana, including direct quotes, is gathered from the following sources: Jim Meenan, "1,400 Monaco Jobs Lost," *South Bend Tribune*, July 18, 2008; James Kelleher, "Economy Slams Brakes on Winnebago," *Global and Mail* (Canada), July 22, 2008; Jim Meenan, "Monaco Says State Requirements Met," *South Bend Tribune*, August 9, 2008; Tony Pugh, "Is RV Capital of America on the Road to Ruin?," *Knight Ridder Washington Bureau*, December 19, 2008; Andrea Holecek, "Notices of Closings or Layoffs Tell Sad Story in Indiana," *Times* (Munster, IN), August 11, 2008; "Corporate Fact Sheet," Monaco Coach Corporation, http://media .corporate-ir.net/media_files/IROL/67/67879/Monaco_factsheet10.11.06.pdf; Joseph Dits, "Agency Leaders Digest the News," *South Bend Tribune*, July 18, 2008.

2. Foreclosure numbers from CoreLogic Press Release, "CoreLogic Reports 61,000 Completed Foreclosures in January," February 28, 2013, http://www.corelogic.com /about-us/news/corelogic-reports-61,000-completed-foreclosures-in-january.aspx. Income destruction figure based on a linear projection of long-term trend growth in GDP according to NIPA data.

3. Suicide risk study is Timothy Classen and Richard A. Dunn, "The Effect of Job Loss and Unemployment Duration on Suicide Risk in the United States: A New Look Using Mass-Layoffs and Unemployment Duration," *Health Economics* 21 (2011): 338–50; Loss earnings study is Steven J. Davis and Till von Wachter, "Recessions and the Costs of Job Loss," *Brookings Papers on Economic Activity*, Fall 2011.

4. Franklin Delano Roosevelt, "Fireside Chat," September 30, 1934.

5. John Maynard Keynes, *The General Theory of Employment, Interest, and Money* (1935; reprint, CreateSpace Independent Publishing Platform, 2011).

6. Arthur Conan Doyle, "A Scandal in Bohemia," in *The Adventures of Sherlock Holmes* (London: George Newnes Ltd., 1892), http://168.144.50.205/221bcollection /canon/scan.htm.

7. David Beim, "It's All about Debt," *Forbes*, March 19, 2009, http://www.forbes.com/2009/03/19/household-debt-gdp-markets-beim.html.

8. Charles Persons, "Credit Expansion, 1920 to 1929, and Its Lessons," *Quarterly Journal of Economics* 45 (1930): 94–130.

9. Martha Olney, "Avoiding Default: The Role of Credit in the Consumption Collapse of 1930," *Quarterly Journal of Economics* 114 (1999): 319–35.

10. Barry Eichengreen and Kris Mitchener, "The Great Depression as a Credit Boom Gone Wrong," *Bank for International Settlements Working Paper* 137 (2003): 36.

11. Olney, "Avoiding Default," 321; Frederic Mishkin, "The Household Balance Sheet and the Great Depression," *Journal of Economic History* 38 (1978): 918–37.

12. Persons, "Credit Expansion."

13. Peter Temin, *Did Monetary Forces Cause the Great Depression?* (New York: Norton, 1976).

14. Reuven Glick and Kevin J. Lansing, "Global Household Leverage, House Prices, and Consumption," *Federal Reserve Bank of San Francisco Economic Letter*, January 11, 2010.

15. International Monetary Fund, "Chapter 3: Dealing with Household Debt," in *World Economic Outlook: Growth Resuming, Dangers Remain*, April 2012.

16. Mervyn King, "Debt Deflation: Theory and Evidence," *European Economic Review* 38 (1994): 419–45.

17. Carmen Reinhart and Kenneth Rogoff, "Is the 2007 US Sub-Prime Financial Crisis So Different?: An International Historical Comparison," *American Economic Review* 98 (2008): 339–44.

18. Carmen Reinhart and Kenneth Rogoff, *This Time Is Different* (Princeton, NJ: Princeton University Press, 2009).

19. Oscar Jorda, Moritz Schularick, and Alan M. Taylor, "When Credit Bites Back: Leverage, Business Cycles, and Crisis" (working paper no. 17621, NBER, 2011).

20. The IMF study also confirms this. They show that elevated household debt leads to more severe recession, even in the absence of a banking crisis. IMF, "Chapter 3: Dealing with Household Debt."

21. Jorda, Schularick, and Taylor, "When Credit Bites Back," 5.

22. George W. Bush, "Speech to the Nation on the Economic Crisis," September 24, 2008, http://www.nytimes.com/2008/09/24/business/economy/24text-bush.html?pagewanted=all&_r=0.

CHAPTER TWO

1. All of the figures in this subsection are from the Survey of Consumer Finances produced by the Board of Governors of the Federal Reserve System.

2. The leverage multiplier is mathematically defined as $1/(1 - LTV)$, where LTV is the loan-to-value ratio on the home. In this example, the LTV was 80 percent, which puts $1/(1 - .80) = 5$. The higher the LTV, the higher the leverage multiplier.

3. For a comprehensive summary of the data sources we have used in our research,

see the following studies: Atif Mian and Amir Sufi, "The Consequences of Mortgage Credit Expansion: Evidence from the U.S. Mortgage Default Crisis," *Quarterly Journal of Economics* 124 (2009): 1449–96; Atif Mian and Amir Sufi, "Household Leverage and the Recession of 2007–2009," *IMF Economic Review* 58 (2010): 74–117; and Atif Mian, Kamelesh Rao, and Amir Sufi, "Household Balance Sheets, Consumption, and the Economic Slump," *Quarterly Journal of Economics*, forthcoming.

4. CoreLogic Press Release, "CoreLogic Third Quarter 2011 Negative Equity Data Shows Slight Decline but Remains Elevated," November 29, 2011, http://www.core logic.com/about-us/news/corelogic-third-quarter-2011-negative-equity-data-shows -slight-decline-but-remains-elevated.aspx.

5. Daniel Hartley, "Distressed Sales and Housing Prices," *Federal Reserve Bank of Cleveland Economic Trends*, February 24, 2012.

6. Atif Mian, Amir Sufi, and Francesco Trebbi, "Foreclosures, House Prices, and the Real Economy" (working paper no. 16685, NBER, May 2012).

7. Another study using a different methodology found very similar results: Elliot Anenberg and Edward Kung, "Estimates of the Size and Source of Price Declines Due to Nearby Foreclosures" (working paper 2013-09, UCLA, January 11, 2013). They find the same channel: foreclosures push down nearby house prices by forcing them to sell below the price previously posted in the market.

8. Andrei Shleifer and Robert Vishny, "Liquidation Values and Debt Capacity: A Market Equilibrium Approach," *Journal of Finance* 47 (1992): 1343–66.

9. John Geanakoplos, "The Leverage Cycle," in *NBER Macroeconomic Annual 2009*, vol. 24, ed. Daron Acemoglu, Kenneth Rogoff, and Michael Woodford (Chicago: University of Chicago Press, 2010), 1–65.

10. See National Fire Protection Association data, http://www.nfpa.org/research /fire-statistics/the-us-fire-problem/home-fires.

CHAPTER THREE

1. The exact quote comes from Alan Blinder, who wrote that the failure to save Lehman "was a colossal error, and many people said so at the time." See Alan Blinder, "Six Errors on the Path to the Financial Crisis," *New York Times*, January 25, 2009.

2. Jacob Weisberg, "What Caused the Great Recession?," *Daily Beast*, January 8, 2010, http://www.thedailybeast.com/newsweek/2010/01/08/what-caused-the-great-reces sion.html.

3. The facts in this section are based on two research studies: Atif Mian, Kamalesh Rao, and Amir Sufi, "Household Balance Sheets, Consumption, and the Economic Slump," *Quarterly Journal of Economics*, forthcoming; and Atif Mian and Amir Sufi, "Household Leverage and the Recession of 2007–2009," *IMF Economic Review* 58 (2010): 74–117.

4. James Surowiecki, "The Deleveraging Myth," *New Yorker*, November 14, 2011. He also wrote in his column that "borrowing furiously against home equity to fuel

a spending spree wasn't sustainable, and we shouldn't be looking to get the economy back to that state." We wholeheartedly agree with this view—see chapters 6 through 8.

5. Karen Dynan at the Brookings Institution also found a strong effect of debt on household spending using a completely different research design and data set. Her analysis found that "highly leveraged homeowners had larger declines in spending between 2007 and 2009 than other homeowners, despite having smaller changes in net worth, suggesting that their leverage weighed on consumption above and beyond what would have been predicted by wealth effects alone." Karen Dynan, "Is a Household Debt Overhang Holding Back Consumption?" *Brookings Papers on Economic Activity* (Spring 2012): 299–344.

CHAPTER FOUR

1. Hal Varian interviews from two sources: Holly Finn, "Lunch with Hal," *Google Think Quarterly*, March 2011, http://www.thinkwithgoogle.co.uk/quarterly/data/hal -varian-treating-data-obesity.html; and McKinsey & Company, "Hal Varian on How the Web Challenges Managers," *McKinsey Quarterly*, January 2009, http://www.mckinsey .com/insights/innovation/hal_varian_on_how_the_web_challenges_managers.

2. Macroeconomists refer to this fundamentals-based theory as *real business cycle theory*, because fluctuations are driven by "real" shocks—that is, shocks to the productive capacity of the economy. The classic citation is Edward C. Prescott, "Theory Ahead of Business Cycle Measurement," *Federal Reserve Bank of Minneapolis Quarterly Review* 10, no. 4 (1986): 9–21.

3. Robert Barro uses this example in chapter 2 of his textbook *Macroeconomics*, 5th ed. (Cambridge, MA: MIT Press, 1997).

4. In addition to our own work, four studies have influenced our thinking on these issues a great deal: Gauti Eggertsson and Paul Krugman, "Debt, Deleveraging, and the Liquidity Trap," *Quarterly Journal of Economics* 127, no. 3 (2012): 1469–513; Veronica Guerrieri and Guido Lorenzoni, "Credit Crises, Precautionary Savings, and the Liquidity Trap" (working paper, University of Chicago Booth School of Business, July 2011); Robert E. Hall, "The Long Slump," *American Economic Review* 101 (2011): 431–69; and Virgiliu Midrigan and Thomas Philippon, "Household Leverage and the Recession" (working paper, NYU Stern School of Business, April 2011).

5. A closely related reason for a pullback in spending after a wealth shock is precautionary savings, as in Christopher Carroll and Miles Kimball, "On the Concavity of the Consumption Function," *Econometrica* 64 (1996): 981–92. Christopher Carroll has done a large amount of work exploring how wealth distribution matters for the pullback in spending during recessions. Related here is also the work of Richard Koo on what he calls the "balance sheet recession" in Japan, where indebted firms pull back on investment to deleverage. See Richard Koo, *The Holy Grail of Macroeconomics: Lessons from Japan's Great Recession* (Singapore: John Wiley & Sons [Asia], 2009).

6. See Paul Krugman, "It's Baaack: Japan's Slump and the Return of the Liquidity Trap," *Brookings Papers on Economic Activity* 2 (1998): 137–205.

7. In theory, cash could have a negative return if the government, or Federal Reserve, taxed it. For example, the Federal Reserve could tax reserves held by banks. In practice, we almost never see such an action, which means the zero lower bound on nominal interest rate remains relevant.

8. Robert Hall explains the intuition of the zero lower bound nicely when he says: "A government issuing currency with a return [higher than the negative real interest rate] is doing something fundamentally uneconomic that no private organization would do—it is overcompensating people who lend to it." In other words, cash becomes an inefficiently high yielding asset, which leads to too much hoarding of it. See Robert E. Hall, "The Long Slump," *American Economic Review* 101 (2011): 431–69.

9. Irving Fisher, "The Debt-Deflation Theory of Great Depressions," *Econometrica* 1 no. 4 (1933): 337–57.

10. For example, Zhen Huo and Jose-Victor Rios-Rull build an economic model in which a recession is generated when wealth is destroyed because it is difficult to shift resources to the production of goods for export. Zhen Huo and Jose-Victor Rios-Rull, "Engineering a Paradox of Thrift Recession" (working paper, University of Minnesota, Minneapolis, December 2012).

11. We build this formal model in Atif Mian and Amir Sufi, "What Explains High Unemployment?: The Aggregate Demand Channel" (working paper, University of Chicago Booth School of Business, 2012).

CHAPTER FIVE

1. Senator Bob Corker, "Corker: Obama Administration's Principal Write-Down Proposal for Underwater Home Mortgages Is 'Terrible Public Policy,' Forces Tennesseans to Pay for Reckless Housing Practices in Other States," press release, January 30, 2012, http://www.corker.senate.gov/public/index.cfm/2012/1/corker-obama-administration-s-principal-write-down-proposal-for-underwater-home-mortgages-is-terrible-public-policy-forces-tennesseans-to-pay-for-reckless-housing-practices-in-other-states.

2. This methodology is based on our research study: Atif Mian and Amir Sufi, "What Explains High Unemployment?: The Aggregate Demand Channel" (working paper, University of Chicago Booth School of Business, 2012).

3. The most important of these assumptions is related to household preferences, where we assume households have Cobb-Douglas preferences over tradable and nontradable goods. This assumption allows for a simple proportionality calculation. The fraction of jobs losses in the *non-tradable* sector coming from the levered losses shock allows us to back out the fraction of total jobs lost in the whole economy. See Atif Mian and Amir Sufi, "What Explains High Unemployment?: The Aggregate Demand Channel."

4. John Maynard Keynes, *The General Theory of Employment, Interest, and Money* (1935; reprint, CreateSpace Independent Publishing Platform, 2011).

5. Mary Daly, Bart Hobijn, and Brian Lucking, "Why Has Wage Growth Stayed Strong?" *FRBSF Economic Letter,* April 2, 2012.

6. Mary Anastasia O'Grady, "The Fed's Easy Money Skeptic," *Wall Street Journal*, February 12, 2011.

7. Kyle Herkenhoff and Lee Ohanian, "Foreclosure Delay and U.S. Unemployment" (working paper, Federal Reserve Bank of St. Louis, June 2012).

8. Jesse Rothstein, "Unemployment Insurance and Job Search in the Great Recession," *Brookings Papers on Economic Activity*, Fall 2011, 143–96.

9. Johannes Schmieder, Till von Wachter, and Stefan Bender, "The Effects of Extended Unemployment Insurance over the Business Cycle: Evidence from Regression Discontinuity Estimates over 20 Years," *Quarterly Journal of Economics* 127 (2012): 701–52.

10. Steven J. Davis and Till von Wachter, "Recessions and the Costs of Job Loss," *Brookings Papers on Economic Activity*, Fall 2011.

CHAPTER SIX

1. We define the west side of Detroit as people living in the following zip codes: 48219, 48223, 48227, 48228, 48235. Background information is from the *Wikipedia* entry on Brightmoor, http://en.wikipedia.org/wiki/Brightmoor,_Detroit, and authors' calculations.

2. Ron French, "How the Home Loan Boom Went Bust," *Detroit News*, November 27, 2007.

3. Mark Whitehouse, "'Subprime' Aftermath: Losing the Family Home," *Wall Street Journal*, May 30, 2007.

4. French, "Home Loan Boom Went Bust."

5. Highest and lowest in this calculation are the top and bottom 20 percent of the credit score distribution, and the denial rates are as of 1998.

6. Ben Bernanke, testimony on "The Economic Outlook" on October 20, 2005, before the Joint Economic Committee, 109th Congress.

7. For details on these calculations, see Atif Mian and Amir Sufi, "The Consequences of Mortgage Credit Expansion: Evidence from the U.S. Mortgage Default Crisis," *Quarterly Journal of Economics* 124 (2009): 1449–96.

8. In reality, the debt and animal spirits view are not independent. For example, debt may allow those with irrational beliefs to buy homes, a channel that we emphasize in chapter 8.

9. Edward Glaeser, Joseph Gyourko, and Albert Saiz, "Housing Supply and Housing Bubbles," *Journal of Urban Economics* 64 (2008): 198–217, provide the motivation for the use of housing -supply elasticity to generate variation in how bubbly a housing market is.

10. Mian and Sufi, "Consequences of Mortgage Credit Expansion"; Albert Saiz, "The Geographic Determinants of Housing Supply," *Quarterly Journal of Economics* 125 (2010): 1253–96.

11. We have on purpose set the y axis labels to match the y axis labels from fig. 6.2. This allows for a direct comparison between inelastic and elastic housing-supply cities.

12. The expansion of credit availability allowed some existing home owners to buy bigger homes, but this represented a small part of the population.

13. See Ron French and Mike Wilkinson, "Easy Money, Risky Loans Drive Area Home Losses; 70,000 Filings for Foreclosure in the Past Two Years," *Detroit News*, November 27, 2007. The article notes that Ms. Cochran was tricked by mortgage brokers into refinancing her mortgage into such a large balance.

14. Atif Mian and Amir Sufi, "House Prices, Home Equity-Based Borrowing, and the U.S. Household Leverage Crisis," *American Economic Review* 101 (2011): 1232–56.

15. Glenn Canner, Karen Dynan, and Wayne Passmore, "Mortgage Refinancing in 2001 and Early 2002," *Federal Reserve Bulletin* 88, no. 12 (2002): 469–81.

16. Other research shows similar aggressive borrowing in the context of credit cards and subprime auto sales. See David Gross and Nicholas Souleles, "Do Liquidity Constraints and Interest Rates Matter for Consumer Behavior?: Evidence from Credit Card Data," *Quarterly Journal of Economics*, no. 117 (2002): 149–85; and William Adams, Liran Einav, and Jonathan Levin, "Liquidity Constraints and Imperfect Information in Subprime Lending," *American Economic Review* no. 99 (2009): 49–84.

17. See, for example, R. H. Strotz, "Myopia and Inconsistency in Dynamic Utility Maximization," *Review of Economic Studies* 3 (1955): 165–80; E. S. Phelps and R. A. Pollak, "On Second-Best National Saving and Game-Equilibrium Growth," *Review of Economic Studies* 35 (1968): 185–99; and David Laibson, "Golden Eggs and Hyperbolic Discounting," *Quarterly Journal of Economics* 112 (1997): 443–78.

18. Distinguishing the borrowing constraints theory from the behavioral biases view remains one of the biggest challenges in the study of household spending behavior. The problem is that observed behavior is almost identical under both theories. Despite the challenges, it remains one of the most important issues in macroeconomics, and we expect to see progress on this question in the future.

CHAPTER SEVEN

1. Laurids Lauridsen, "The Financial Crisis in Thailand: Causes, Conduct, and Consequences?" *World Development* 26 (1998): 1575–91.

2. Lester Thurow, "Asia: The Collapse and the Cure," *New York Review of Books*, February 5, 1998.

3. Ramon Moreno, "What Caused East Asia's Financial Crisis?" *Federal Reserve Bank of San Francisco Economic Letter* 98-24, August 7, 1998.

4. Paul Krugman, "What Happened to Asia," *Mimeo*, January 1998, http://web.mit.edu/krugman/www/disinter.html.

5. Franklin Allen and Joo Yun Hong, "Why Are There Global Imbalances?: The Case of Korea" (working paper 11-32, Wharton Financial Institutions Center, University of Pennsylvania, February 27, 2011).

6. Leon Kendall, "Securitization: A New Era in American Finance," in *A Primer on Securitization*, ed. Leon Kendall and Michael Fishman (Cambridge, MA: MIT Press, 2000).

7. See, for example, Claire Hill, "Who Were the Villains in the Subprime Crisis, and Why It Matters," *Entrepreneurial Business Law Journal* 4 (2010): 323–50. As she notes, "In the late 1990s, Wall Street began securitizing mortgages made to borrowers who did not have 'prime' credit. Origination of such mortgages had been a very small proportion of overall mortgage originations, but that quickly began to change."

8. Adam Levitin and Susan Wachter, "Explaining the Housing Bubble," *Georgetown Law Journal* 100 (2012): 1177–258.

9. Joshua Coval, Jakub Jurek, and Erik Stafford, "The Economics of Structured Finance," *Journal of Economic Perspectives* 23 (2009): 3–25.

10. Coval, Jurek, and Stafford, "The Economics of Structured Finance."

11. This was the title of an *Economist* article that covered our research in February 2008. See the *Economist*, "Chain of Fools," February 7, 2008.

12. Benjamin Keys, T. Mukherjee, Amit Seru, and Vikrant Vig, "Did Securitization Lead to Lax Screening?: Evidence from Subprime Loans," *Quarterly Journal of Economics* 125 (2010): 307–62.

13. Christopher Mayer, Karen Pence, and Shane Sherlund, "The Rise in Mortgage Defaults," *Journal of Political Economy* 23 (2009): 27–50, provide further support. They "find that underwriting deteriorated along several dimensions: more loans were originated to borrowers with very small down payments and little or no documentation of their income or assets, in particular."

14. Tomasz Piskorski, Amit Seru, and James Witkin, "Asset Quality Misrepresentation by Financial Intermediaries: Evidence from RMBS Market" (working paper, Columbia Business School, Columbia University, February 12, 2013).

15. Adam Ashcraft, Paul Goldsmith-Pinkham, and James Vickery, "MBS Ratings and the Mortgage Credit Boom," *Federal Reserve Bank of New York Staff Report #449*, May 2010.

16. Piskorski, Seru, and Witkin, "Asset Quality Misrepresentation."

17. Yuliya Demyanyk and Otto Van Hemert, "Understanding the Subprime Mortgage Crisis," *Review of Financial Studies* 24 (2011): 1848–80.

18. This estimate is based on the ABX index that tracks the value of mortgage-backed securities with mortgage originated in 2007.

CHAPTER EIGHT

1. Daniel Altman, "Charles P. Kindleberger, 92, Global Economist, Is Dead," *New York Times*, July 9, 2003.

2. Robert Solow, foreword to *Manias, Panics, and Crashes: A History of Financial Crises*, 5th ed., by Charles Kindleberger and Robert Aliber (Hoboken, NJ: John Wiley & Sons, 2005).

3. Vernon Smith, Gerry Suchanek, and Arlington Williams, "Bubbles, Crashes and Endogenous Expectations in Experimental Spot Asset Markets," *Econometrica* 56 (1988): 1119–51.

4. Robert Shiller, "Do Stock Prices Move Too Much to Be Justified by Subsequent Changes in Dividends?" *American Economic Review* 71 (1981): 421–36.

5. Jeffrey Pontiff, "Excess Volatility and Closed-End Funds," *American Economic Review* 87 (1997): 155–69.

6. David Porter and Vernon Smith, "Stock Market Bubbles in the Laboratory," *Journal of Behavioral Finance* 4 (2003): 7–20.

7. See the following studies for models describing this logic: Michael Harrison and David Kreps, "Speculative Investor Behavior in a Stock Market with Heterogeneous Expectations," *Quarterly Journal of Economics* 92 (1978): 323–36; Jose Scheinkman and Wei Xiong, "Overconfidence and Speculative Bubbles," *Journal of Political Economy* 111 (2003): 1183–219; and Dilip Abreu and Markus Brunnermeier, "Bubbles and Crashes," *Econometrica* 71 (2003): 173–204.

8. The discussion below is inspired by John Geanakoplos, "The Leverage Cycle," in *NBER Macroeconomic Annual 2009*, vol. 24, ed. Daron Acemoglu, Kenneth Rogoff, and Michael Woodford (Chicago: University of Chicago Press, 2010), 1–65.

9. This can be confirmed by noting that $100 \times \$125{,}000 = \$12.5$ million.

10. See, for example, Edward Glaeser, Joshua Gottlieb, and Joseph Gyourko, "Can Cheap Credit Explain the Housing Boom?" (working paper no. 16230, NBER, July 2010).

11. Nicola Gennaioli, Andrei Shleifer, and Robert Vishny, "Neglected Risks, Financial Innovation, and Financial Fragility," *Journal of Financial Economics* 104 (2012): 452–68.

12. Solow, foreword to *Manias, Panics and Crashes*.

13. Jon Hilsenrath, "A 91-Year-Old Who Foresaw Selloff is 'Dubious' of Stock-Market Rally," *Wall Street Journal*, July 25, 2002.

CHAPTER NINE

1. *Euronews*, "Spain's Unforgiving Eviction Law," December 11, 2012; Suzanne Daley, "In Spain, Homes Are Taken but Debt Stays," *New York Times*, October 27, 2010.

2. Gabriele Steinhauser and Matthew Dalton, "Lingering Bad Debts Stifle Europe Recovery," *Wall Street Journal*, January 31, 2013.

3. Daley, "In Spain, Homes."

4. Matt Moffett and Christopher Bjork, "Wave of Evictions Spurs Sympathy in Spain," *Wall Street Journal*, December 11, 2012.

5. Ilan Brat and Gabrielle Steinhauser, "EU Court Rules against Spanish Mortgage Laws," *Wall Street Journal*, March 14, 2013.

6. *Wall Street Journal*, "Spanish Mortgage Misery," March 21, 2013.

7. Sharon Smyth and Angeline Benoit, "PP Aims to Change Spanish Mortgage Law within Two Months," *Bloomberg*, March 27, 2013.

8. Daley, "In Spain, Homes."

9. Raphael Minder, "Bailout in Spain Leaves Taxpayers Liable for Cost," *New York Times*, June 12, 2012.

10. "Robert Reich," *Daily Show with Jon Stewart*, Comedy Central, October 16, 2008.

11. Stephen G. Cecchetti, "Crisis and Responses: The Federal Reserve in the Early Stages of the Financial Crisis," *Journal of Economic Perspectives* 23, no. 1 (2009).

12. Pietro Veronesi and Luigi Zingales, "Paulson's Gift," *Journal of Financial Economics* 97 (2010): 339–68.

13. Bryan Kelly, Hanno Lustig, and Stijn Van Nieuwerburgh, "Too-Systemic-to-Fail: What Option Markets Imply about Sector-Wide Government Guarantees" (Fama-Miller working paper, University of Chicago Booth School of Business, March 21, 2012).

14. George W. Bush, "Address to the Nation on the Financial Crisis" (speech, Washington, DC, September 24, 2008), *New York Times*, http://www.nytimes.com/2008/09/24/business/economy/24text-bush.html?pagewanted=all&_r=0.

15. Ben Bernanke, "Nonmonetary Effects of the Financial Crisis in the Propagation of the Great Depression," *American Economic Review* 73 (1983): 257–76.

16. The NFIB survey, led by Chief Economist William Dunkelberg, is available at http://www.nfib.com/research-foundation/surveys/small-business-economic-trends.

17. Atif Mian and Amir Sufi, "Aggregate Demand and State-Level Employment," *Federal Reserve Bank of San Francisco Economic Letter 2013-04*, February 11, 2013.

18. Atif Mian and Amir Sufi, "What Explains High Unemployment?: The Aggregate Demand Channel" (working paper, University of Chicago Booth School of Business, 2012).

19. Kathleen Kahle and Rene M. Stulz, "Access to Capital, Investment, and the Financial Crisis," *Journal of Financial Economics*, forthcoming.

20. Atif Mian, Amir Sufi, and Francesco Trebbi, "The Political Economy of the U.S. Mortgage Default Crisis," *American Economic Review* 100 (2010): 67–98.

21. The printed transcript was made available on the *Columbia Journalism Review* website, and is located here: http://www.cjr.org/the_audit/so_thats_why_the_press_wont_co_1.php?page=all&print=true. Davidson later apologized to listeners for this segment of the interview.

22. The question was posed during the London School of Economics conference entitled "What Should Economists and Policymakers Learn from the Financial Crisis?" on March 25, 2013. The transcript is on Brad DeLong's website located here: http://delong.typepad.com/sdj/2013/04/reconstructing-macroeconomics-exchange-mervyn-king-ben-bernanke-olivier-blanchard-axel-weber-larry-summers.html.

23. Clea Benson, "Obama Housing Fix Faltered on Carrots-Not-Sticks Policy," *Bloomberg News*, June 11, 2012.

24. Kristin Roberts and Stacy Kaper, "Out of Their Depth," *National Journal*, March 22, 2012.

CHAPTER TEN

1. CNBC video can be found at the following link: http://video.cnbc.com/gallery/?video=1039849853.

2. Dina ElBoghdady, "HUD Chief Calls Aid on Mortgages a Failure," *Washington Post*, December 17, 2008.

3. SIGTARP, "Quarterly Report to Congress," April 24, 2013, http://www.sigtarp .gov/Quarterlypercent20Reports/April_24_2013_Report_to_Congress.pdf.

4. Office of the Special Inspector General for the Troubled Asset Relief Program, "Quarterly Report to Congress," April 24, 2013. Available at http://www.sigtarp.gov /Quarterly%20Reports/April_24_2013_Report_to_Congress.pdf.

5. Zachary Goldfarb, "Why Housing Is Still Hindering the Recovery," *Washington Post*, November 24, 2012.

6. Kristin Roberts and Stacy Kaper, "Out of Their Depth," *National Journal*, March 22, 2012.

7. See, in particular, Anna Gelpern and Adam Levitin, "Rewriting Frankenstein Contracts: Workout Prohibitions in Residential Mortgage-Backed Securities," *Southern California Law Review* 82 (2009): 1075–152.

8. Ibid.

9. Ibid.

10. John Geanakoplos, "Solving the Present Crisis and Managing the Leverage Cycle," *FRBNY Economic Policy Review* 16, no. 1 (August 2010).

11. Christopher Mayer, Edward Morrison, and Tomasz Piskorski, "A New Proposal for Loan Modifications," *Yale Journal on Regulation* 26, no. 2 (2009).

12. Sumit Agarwal, Gene Amromin, Itzhak Ben-David, Souphala Chomsisengphet, Tomasz Piskorski, and Amit Seru, "Policy Intervention in Debt Renegotiation: Evidence from the Home Affordable Modification Program" (working paper, University of Chicago Booth School of Business, 2012).

13. Tomasz Piskorski, Amit Seru, and Vikrant Vig, "Securitization and Distressed Loan Renegotiation: Evidence from the Subprime Mortgage Crisis," *Journal of Financial Economics* 97 (2010): 369–97.

14. Sumit Agarwal, Gene Amromin, Itzhak Ben-David, Souphala Chomsisengphet, and Douglas Evanoff, "Market-Based Loss Mitigation Practices for Troubled Mortgages Following the Financial Crisis," (working paper, SSRN, October 2010).

15. Research by Christopher Mayer, Edward Morrison, Tomasz Piskorski, and Arpit Gupta, "Mortgage Modification and Strategic Behavior: Evidence from a Legal Settlement with Countrywide" (working paper no. 17065, NBER, May 2011), provides support to these strategic default concerns.

16. See Jesse Eisenger, "Fannie and Freddie: Slashing Mortgages Is Good Business," *ProPublica*, March 23, 2012, http://www.propublica.org/article/fannie-and-freddie -slashing-mortgages-is-good-business.

17. See Ben Hallman, "Ed DeMarco, Top Housing Official, Defied White House; Geithner Fires Back," *Huffington Post*, July 31, 2012, http://www.huffingtonpost .com/2012/07/31/ed-demarco-principal-reduction_n_1724880.html.

18. Annie Lowrey, "White House Urged to Fire a Housing Regulator," *New York Times*, March 17, 2013.

19. See interview with Mike Konczal of *Next New Deal*, http://www.nextnewdeal .net/rortybomb/post-debate-interview-glenn-hubbard-housing-policy.

20. The general insight is that in the presence of nominal rigidities, financial market outcomes may be inefficient because of an aggregate demand externality. See Emmanuel Farhi and Ivan Werning, "On the Inefficiency of Financial Market Equilibria in Macroeconomic Models with Nominal Rigidities" (working paper, Harvard University, 2013). As they show, transfers such as the one we propose make sense.

21. For example, a common counterargument goes something like this: There was $750 billion of underwater mortgage debt. Even if the indebted households were given this $750 billion, they would have spent only $0.10 on the dollar, which is only $75 billion. This is small relative to total GDP. However, such a calculation ignores the knock-on effects of foreclosures on house prices and the knock-on effects on employment, which as we explained in chapter 5 were very large.

22. Martin Feldstein, "How to Stop the Drop in Home Values," *New York Times*, October 12, 2011.

23. Goldfarb, "Why Housing Is Still Hindering the Recovery."

24. Craig Torres, "Household Debt Restructuring in U.S. Would Stimulate Growth, Reinhart Says," *Bloomberg*, August 5, 2011.

25. Murray N. Rothbard, *The Panic of 1819: Reactions and Policies* (New York: Columbia University Press, 1962), 7.

26. Patrick Bolton and Howard Rosenthal, "Political Intervention in Debt Contracts," *Journal of Political Economy* 110 (2002): 1103–34.

27. Rothbard, *Panic of 1819*, 24.

28. Bolton and Rosenthal, "Political Intervention."

29. Rothbard, *Panic of 1819*.

30. Ibid.

31. Ibid., 28.

32. Price Fishback, Jonathan Rose, and Kenneth Snowden, *Well Worth Saving: How the New Deal Safeguarded Home Ownership* (Chicago: University of Chicago Press, 2013).

33. Ibid.

34. Randall Kroszner, "Is It Better to Forgive than to Receive?: Repudiation of the Gold Indexation Clause in Long-Term Debt during the Great Depression" (manuscript, University of Chicago, 1998).

35. John Geanakoplos and Susan Koniak, "Mortgage Justice Is Blind," *New York Times*, October 29, 2008.

36. Information on Chapter 13 bankruptcy comes from Mark Scarberry and Scott Reddie, "Home Mortgage Strip Down in Chapter 13 Bankruptcy: A Contextual Approach to Sections 1322(b)(2) and (b)(5)," *Pepperdine Law Review* 20, no. 2 (2012): 425–96.

37. There is considerable legal controversy on this interpretation. A series of cases in the late 1980s and early 1990s ended with *Nobleman v. American Savings Bank* in 1992. The court ruled that secured mortgage debt on a principal residence could not

NOTES TO PAGES 146–153 **203**

be written down according to the original Chapter 13 bankruptcy statute. Before then, many judges allowed for mortgage cram-down in bankruptcy. Scarberry and Reddie, "Home Mortgage Strip Down in Chapter 13 Bankruptcy."

38. Clea Benson, "Obama Housing Fix Faltered on Carrots-Not-Sticks Policy," *Bloomberg News*, June 11, 2012.

39. Binyamin Appelbaum, "Cautious Moves on Foreclosures Haunting Obama," *New York Times*, August 19, 2012.

40. Ibid.

41. Doris Dungey, "Just Say Yes to Cram Downs," *Calculated Risk*, October 7, 2007, http://www.calculatedriskblog.com/2007/10/just-say-yes-to-cram-downs.html.

42. Doris Dungey, "House Considers Cram Downs," *Calculated Risk*, December 12, 2007, http://www.calculatedriskblog.com/2007/12/house-considers-cram-downs.html.

43. Bill McBride, "Mortgage Cramdowns: A Missed Opportunity," *Calculated Risk*, August 20, 2012, http://www.calculatedriskblog.com/2012/08/mortgage-cramdowns-missed-opportunity.html.

44. A related proposal came from Eric Posner and Luigi Zingales that would have modified Chapter 13 to allow home owners in zip codes especially hard hit by falling house prices to have mortgages written down in bankruptcy if they gave up some of the upside potential when they sold the home in the future. See Eric Posner and Luigi Zingales, "A Loan Modification Approach to the Housing Crisis," *American Law and Economics Review* 11, no. 2 (2009): 575–607.

45. See Geanakoplos, "Solving the Present Crisis."

46. OCC Mortgage Metrics Report, "OCC Reports on Mortgage Performance for Fourth Quarter," March 27, 2013.

47. Roberts and Kaper, "Out of Their Depth."

48. Benson, "Obama Housing Fix Faltered."

49. International Monetary Fund, "Concluding Statement of the 2012 Article IV Mission to the United States of America," July 3, 2012, http://www.imf.org/external/np/ms/2012/070312.htm.

50. Daniel Leigh, Deniz Igan, John Simon, and Petia Topalova, "Chapter 3: Dealing with Household Debt," in *IMF World Economic Outlook: Growth Resuming, Dangers Remain*, April 2012.

51. Will Dobbie and Jae Song, "Debt Relief and Debtor Outcomes: Measuring the Effects of Consumer Bankruptcy Protection" (working paper, Harvard University, May 2013).

CHAPTER ELEVEN

1. Irving Fisher, "The Debt-Deflation Theory of Great Depressions," *Econometrica* 1 no. 4 (1933): 341.

2. Ben Bernanke, "On Milton Friedman's Ninetieth Birthday" (speech, Conference to Honor Milton Friedman, University of Chicago, November 8, 2002).

3. Technically, the Federal Reserve also purchases securities from the non-bank public. But if the non-bank public deposit the proceeds into the banking system and the banking system holds the increased funds in reserves, then the implications are similar.

4. Paul Douglas, Irving Fisher, Frank Graham, Earl Hamilton, Willford King, and Charles Whittlesey, "A Program for Monetary Reform" (paper, reprinted by the Kettle Pond Institute, July 1939).

5. Richard Koo makes a similar argument studying Japan during the 1990s. See Richard Koo, *The Holy Grail of Macroeconomics: Lessons from Japan's Great Recession* (Singapore: John Wiley & Sons [Asia], 2009).

6. See Peter Temin, *Did Monetary Forces Cause the Great Depression?* (New York: Norton, 1976); and Paul Krugman, "It's Baaack: Japan's Slump and the Return of the Liquidity Trap," *Brookings Papers on Economic Activity* 2 (1998): 137–205.

7. Richard Koo, "The World in Balance Sheet Recession: What Post-2008 West Can Learn from Japan 1990–2005" (presentation, "Paradigm Lost: Rethinking Economics and Politics" conference, Berlin, April 15, 2012), http://ineteconomics.org/conference /berlin/world-balance-sheet-recession-what-post-2008-west-can-learn-japan-1990 -2005.

8. The most cited reference to such helicopter drops of money is Milton Friedman, "The Optimum Quantity of Money," in *The Optimum Quantity of Money and Other Essays* (Chicago: Aldine, 1969), 1–50.

9. Ben Bernanke, "Japanese Monetary Policy: A Case of Self-Induced Paralysis" (paper, Princeton University, 1999).

10. Martin Wolf, "The Case for Helicopter Money," *Financial Times*, February 12, 2013.

11. Willem H. Buiter, "Helicopter Money: Irredeemable Fiat Money and the Liquidity Trap; Or, Is Money Net Wealth after All?" (working paper, January 31, 2004), http://www.willembuiter.com/helinber.pdf.

12. Alan Boyce, Glenn Hubbard, Christopher Mayer, and James Witkin, "Streamlined Refinancings for Up to 13 Million Borrowers" (draft policy proposal, Columbia Business School, Columbia University, June 13, 2012), http://www8.gsb.columbia.edu /sites/realestate/files/BHMW-V15-post.pdf.

13. Krugman, "It's Baaack."

14. Christina Romer, "It Takes a Regime Shift: Recent Developments in Japanese Monetary Policy through the Lens of the Great Depression" (speech, NBER Annual Conference on Macroeconomics, Cambridge, MA, April 12, 2013).

15. Emi Nakamura and Jon Steinsson, "Fiscal Stimulus in a Monetary Union: Evidence from U.S. Regions," *American Economic Review*, forthcoming.

16. Gabriel Chodorow-Reich, Laura Feiveson, Zachary Liscow, and William Gui Woolston, "Does State Fiscal Relief during Recessions Increase Employment?: Evidence from the American Recovery and Reinvestment Act," *American Economic Journal: Economic Policy* 4 (2012): 118–145; and Daniel Wilson, "Fiscal Spending Job Multi-

pliers: Evidence from the 2009 American Recovery and Reinvestment Act," *Amer.* *Economic Journal: Economic Policy*, forthcoming.

17. Gauti Eggertsson and Paul Krugman, "Debt, Deleveraging, and the Liquidity Trap: A Fisher-Minsky-Koo Approach," *Quarterly Journal of Economics* 127, no. 3 (2012): 1469–513.

18. Paul Krugman, *End This Depression Now!* (New York: Norton, 2012).

19. There are, of course, examples where government spending took the form of principal forgiveness. The most obvious is the Home Owners' Loan Corporation during the Great Depression that we discussed in chapter 10.

20. The estate tax is an exception, but accounts for only 0.6 percent of overall tax revenue. See Center on Budget and Policy Priorities, "Where Do Federal Tax Revenues Come From?" April 12, 2013, http://www.cbpp.org/cms/?fa=view&id=3822.

21. Hans-Werner Sinn, "Why Berlin Is Balking on a Bailout," *New York Times*, June 12, 2012.

22. Atif Mian, Amir Sufi, and Francesco Trebbi, "Resolving Debt Overhang: Political Constraints in the Aftermath of Financial Crises," *American Economic Journal: Macroeconomics*, forthcoming.

23. Ibid.

24. These are financial crises defined by Carmen Reinhart and Ken Rogoff.

CHAPTER TWELVE

1. See Heidi Shierholz, Natalie Sabadish, and Nicholas Finio, "The Class of 2013: Young Graduates Still Face Dim Job Prospects," *Economic Policy Institute Briefing Paper* 360 (2013): 1–30.

2. See Federal Reserve Bank of New York, *Quarterly Report on Household Debt and Credit*, February 2013, http://www.newyorkfed.org/research/national_economy /householdcredit/DistrictReport_Q42012.pdf.

3. Andrew Martin and Andrew Lehren, "A Generation Hobbled by the Soaring Cost of College," *New York Times*, May 12, 2012.

4. Tara Siegel Bernard, "In Grim Job Market, Student Loans Are a Costly Burden," *New York Times*, April 18, 2009.

5. See Charley Stone, Carl Van Horn, and Cliff Zukin, "Chasing the American Dream: Recent College Graduates and the Great Recession," in *Work Trends: Americans' Attitudes about Work, Employers, and Government* (Rutgers University, May 2012), http://media.philly.com/documents/20120510_Chasing_American_Dream.pdf; and Meta Brown and Sydnee Caldwell, "Young Student Loan Borrowers Retreat from Housing and Auto Markets," *Federal Reserve Bank of New York Liberty Street Economics Blog*, April 17, 2013, http://libertystreeteconomics.newyorkfed.org/2013/04/young -student-loan-borrowers-retreat-from-housing-and-auto-markets.html.

6. Martin and Lehren, "A Generation Hobbled."

7. Bernard, "In Grim Job Market."

influenced heavily by the work of Robert Shiller for many of the
er. He has been a strong advocate for financial contracts that more
in the context of household and sovereign debt. See, for example,
ulis, Robert Shiller, and Eric van Wincoop, "Macro Markets and
rity," *FRBNY Economic Policy Review*, April 2009. Kenneth Rogoff has
cated more equity-like instruments in the context of sovereign debt. See
Kenneth Rogoff, "Global Imbalances without Tears," *Project Syndicate*, March 1, 2011,
http://www.project-syndicate.org/commentary/global-imbalances-without-tears.
Lord Adair Turner has summarized excellently the problems with debt and advantages of equity finance. See Lord Adair Turner, "Monetary and Financial Stability:
Lessons from the Crisis and from Classic Economics Texts" (speech at South African
Reserve Bank, November 2, 2012), available at http://www.fsa.gov.uk/static/pubs
/speeches/1102-at.pdf.

9. Many have argued for student education financing to be contingent on income.
See, for example, Kevin Carey, "The U.S. Should Adopt Income-Based Loans Now,"
Chronicle of Higher Education, October 23, 2011; and Bruce Chapman, "A Better Way
to Borrow," *Inside Higher Ed*, June 8, 2010. Elena Del Rey and Maria Racionero argue
that "an income contingent loan with risk-pooling can induce the optimal level of
participation provided that the scheme is universal and the loan covers both financial
costs of education and foregone earnings." See Elena Del Rey and Maria Racionero,
"Financing Schemes for Higher Education," *European Journal of Political Economy* 26
(2010): 104–13.

10. Milton Friedman, "The Role of Government in Education," in *Economics and
the Public Interest*, ed. Robert A Solo (New Brunswick, NJ: Rutgers University Press,
1955), http://www.edchoice.org/The-Friedmans/The-Friedmans-on-School-Choice
/The-Role-of-Government-in-Education- percent281995 percent29.aspx.

11. We are not the first to propose risk-sharing arrangements in mortgage finance.
See, for example, Andrew Caplin, Sewin Chan, Charles Freeman, and Joseph Tracy,
Housing Partnerships (Cambridge, MA: MIT Press, 1997); Andrew Caplin, Noel Cun-
ningham, Mitchell Engler, and Frederick Pollock, "Facilitating Shared Appreciation
Mortgages to Prevent Housing Crashes and Affordability Crises" (discussion paper
2008-12, Hamilton Project, September 2008); and David Miles, "Housing, Leverage,
and Stability in the Wider Economy" (speech at the Housing Stability and Macro-
economy: International Perspectives Conference, Federal Reserve Bank of Dallas,
November 2013), available at http://www.bankofengland.co.uk/publications/Pages
/news/2013/132.aspx.

12. This is a *yearly* mortgage payment, not a monthly one.

13. If the mortgage payment were linked to the exact value of Jane's house, she
would have a perverse incentive to hurt the home's value through neglect in order
to reduce the payment. This moral hazard problem is important and explains why
equity-like contracts should be made contingent on a measure of asset performance
outside the control of the borrower.

14. CoreLogic estimates $822 billion in negative equity of 12.1 million home owners

in the first quarter of 2010. Our debt write-off is significantly less because the dec.. in house prices is less severe in the SRM scenario with the avoidance of foreclosures.

15. See also Xia Zhou and Christopher Carroll, "Dynamics of Wealth and Consumption: New and Improved Measures for U.S. States," *B.E. Journal of Macroeconomics* 12, no. 2 (2012).

16. Nakamura and Steinsson, "Fiscal Stimulus in a Monetary Union."

17. Frank Fabozzi and Franco Modigliani, *Mortgage and Mortgage-Backed Securities Markets* (Boston: Harvard Business School Press, 1992).

18. Miles, "Housing, Leverage, and Stability in the Wider Economy."

19. See Gregor Matvos and Zhiguo He, "Debt and Creative Destruction: Why Could Subsidizing Corporate Debt Be Optimal?" (working paper, University of Chicago Booth School of Business, March 2013).

20. See Pierre-Olivier Gourinchas and Olivier Jeanne, "Global Safe Assets" (Bank for International Settlements working paper 399, December 2012). As they note, "Privately produced stores of value cannot provide sufficient insurance against global shocks. Only public safe assets may, if appropriately supported by monetary policy."

21. Annette Krishnamurthy and Arvind Krishnamurthy, "Short-Term Debt and Financial Crisis: What Can We Learn from U.S. Treasury Supply" (working paper, Kellogg School of Management, Northwestern University, May 2013).

22. Mark Kamstra and Robert Shiller, "The Case for Trills: Giving the People and Their Pension Funds a Stake in the Wealth of the Nation" (discussion paper No. 1717, Cowles Foundation, Yale University, August 2009).

23. Rogoff, "Global Imbalances without Tears"

24. Anat Admati and Martin Hellwig, *The Bankers' New Clothes: What's Wrong with Banking and What to Do about It* (Princeton, NJ: Princeton University Press, 2013).

INDEX

housing boom of 2000–2007 (*continued*) 51, 164–65; international markets and, 92–95; mortgage credit expansion of, 75–91, 164–65; refinancing during, 158–59; in Spain, 119–21; in Tennessee, 60–61

housing crash. *See* collapse in housing prices; Great Recession

housing supply: elasticity of, 82–85, 196n11; lending boom and, 92

housing-wealth effect, 38–42, 88–89, 176

Hubbard, Glenn, 140

human consequences of unemployment, 2–3, 70

Huo, Zhen, 195n10

hyperbolic consumers, 90–91, 197n18

income, 174. *See also* wages

income destruction, 2, 191n2

income taxes, 164

inelastic housing supply, 82–87, 196n11

inequality (in wealth), 19–21, 23–25, 45, 71

inflation, 54–55, 153–62; currency injections and, 153–57; expectations of, 160–62; interest-rate manipulation and, 158–59

installment financing, 5

insurance, 17, 30

interest rates: banking system stress and, 129, 130f; Federal Reserve manipulation of, 158–59; in fundamentals view of recession, 52–53, 124–25; IMF loan policies and, 94–95; negative returns in, 53–55, 161, 195n7; zero lower bound in, 53–56, 67, 154, 195n8

International Monetary Fund (IMF), 192n29; East Asian bailouts by, 94–95; on household debt and spending, 6–7; on household-debt restructuring, 148; voting power in, 94

investment, 32–35. *See also* residential investment

investor-purchased properties, 102–3

investors. *See* mortgage lenders; savers

irrational behavior, 90–91, 111–13

It's a Wonderful Life, 95, 123

Jorda, Oscar, 8–9

judicial foreclosure, 28, 29f

junior claims, 18–19, 50. *See also* borrowers

Jurek, Jakub, 98, 101

Kahle, Kathleen, 129

Kamstra, Mark, 185

Kaper, Stacy, 134

Kazee, Ezra, 168

Kelly, Bryan, 126

Keynes, John Maynard, 3, 67, 68, 163

Keys, Benjamin, 101–2

Kimball, Miles, 194n5

Kindleberger, Charles P., 106–8, 110, 115–16, 170

King, Mervyn, 7

Koniak, Susan, 145–46

Koo, Richard, 156, 194n5

Krishnamurthy, Arvind, 184

Kroszner, Randall, 145

Krugman, Paul, 92–93, 156, 161, 163

Kung Edward, 193n7

labor migration, 67

Lansing, Kevin, 6, 7

Large-Scale Asset Purchase (LSAP), 125

Lehman Brothers, 31–34, 193n1

Lehren, Andrew, 168

lenders. *See* mortgage lenders; savers

lenders of last resort, 124–26

lending boom, 92–105, 107–8, 113–16, 164–65; appearance of safety in, 98–101, 103, 115, 170; default crisis and, 101–5, 198n18; East Asian capital and, 92–95; home construction boom and, 92; low-credit-score lending of, 76–77, 80–85; myopic consumers and, 90–91, 197n18; originator misrepresentation and, 101–5, 198n13; securitization practices of, 95–101, 198n7. *See also* bubbles; mortgage credit expansion